Workbook

by Lisa Raftery
and Barbara Precourt

Published by
Harrison House Publishing
Tulsa, OK

Mr. Right Series Workbook:
Novels 1, 2 and 3:

Unless otherwise indicated, all Scripture references are taken from the New King James Version of the Bible. Copyright © 1982 by Thomas Nelson, Inc. Used by permission. All rights reserved.

Scripture quotations marked NLT are taken from the Holy Bible, New Living Translation, copyright © 1996, 2004. Used by permission of Tyndale House Publishers, Inc. Wheaton, Illinois 60189. All rights reserved.

Scripture quotations marked AMP are taken from The Amplified Bible, copyright © 1954, 1958, 1962, 1964, 1965, 1987 by the Lockman Foundation. All rights reserved. Used by permission.

Scripture quotations marked NIV are taken from the Holy Bible, New International Version®. NIV®. Copyright © 1973, 1978, 1984 by International Bible Society1973, 1978, 1984 by Biblica. Used by permission. All rights reserved.

Scripture quotations marked (CEV) are from the Contemporary English Version Copyright ©1991, 1992, 1995, by American Bible Society. Used by permission.*

Scripture quotations marked WE are taken from THE JESUS BOOK - The Bible in Worldwide English. Copyright SOON Educational Publications, Derby DE656BN, UK. Used by permission.

Note: Any bolding of Scripture text has been added by the author.

Novel 1 Section:

shame. (2010). ©2002 Wordsmyth. Retrieved January 26, 2010 from http://new.wordsmyth.net/

shame. (2010). *Random House Unabridged Dictionary,* Copyright © 1997, by Random House, Inc., on Infoplease. Retrieved January 26, 2010 from http://dictionary.infoplease.com/shame

pure. (2010). In *Merriam-Webster Online Dictionary.* Retrieved January 26, 2010, from http://www.merriam-webster.com/dictionary/pure

*1 Thessalonians 4:3-5 The word *body* is used here in various translations. In the Contemporary English
Version, it is included in the footnote; the author made the substitution for clarity.

Mr. Right Series Workbook
ISBN: 978-160683829-7
Copyright © 2013 by Lisa Raftery and Barbara Precourt
Published by Harrison House Publishers, Inc.

Cover Photography: Scott Miller, Miller Photography Tulsa, OK
Cover Models: Olivia Ophus and Caleb Ophus
Cover Design: Christian Ophus

Printed in the United States of America. All rights reserved under International Copyright Law. No part of this publication may be reproduced, stored in a retrieval system, or transmitted in any form or by any means, without the express written consent of the Publisher.

Contents

                                                      Page

Welcome vi
How to Use This Workbook vii
Sample Workbook Entry viii
Sample Journal Entry ix

Novel 1: **Waiting for Mr. Right**

    Chapter 1—Unexpected Turn 1
    Chapter 2—Mr. Wonderful 9
    Chapter 3—Failed Attempt 19
    Chapter 4—Facing the Problem 24
    Chapter 5—A Brand New Deal.....................29
    Chapter 6—Awakened Desire......................36
    Chapter 7—Warnings 40
    Chapter 8—Living the Lie........................50
    Chapter 9—Seeing the Truth 53
    Chapter 10—A Night of Regrets 60
    Chapter 11—Making Choices 66
    Chapter 12—Walking Away 79
    Chapter 13—One Last Date 85
    Chapter 14—Heavenly Assistance 92
    Chapter 15—Necessary Consequences 96
    Chapter 16—Girl Talk 100
    Chapter 17—Looking Ahead.......................107

Contents (continued)

Page

Novel 2: Meeting Mr. Right

Chapter 1—Starting Over 113
Chapter 2—Bittersweet Reunion 115
Chapter 3—Prince or Pauper? 117
Chapter 4—Beauty Lessons 119
Chapter 5—No More Secrets......................121
Chapter 6—Common Sense 123
Chapter 7—Sister Talk 125
Chapter 8—Unwanted Admirer 127
Chapter 9—Tall Paul 129
Chapter 10—Daffy Dinah 131
Chapter 11—Current Events 133
Chapter 12—S.O.S. Online 135
Chapter 13—Reaching Out 137
Chapter 14—First Kiss 139
Chapter 15—Readjusting the Focus 141
Chapter 16—Risky Business 143
Chapter 17—Staying Strong 145
Chapter 18—Ups and Downs 147
Chapter 19—Internal Affairs 149
Chapter 20—Déjà Vu 151

Contents (continued)

_____Page

Novel 3: **Marrying Mr. Right**

Chapter 1—The Shortcut. 155
Chapter 2—No Answer. 157
Chapter 3—No Fairy Tale 159
Chapter 4—Sending Daisies 161
Chapter 5—A Cinderella Story 163
Chapter 6—The Other Woman 165
Chapter 7—Dinner and a Movie 167
Chapter 8—A Happier Melody 169
Chapter 9—Tradition 171
Chapter 10—On the Terrace 173
Chapter 11—Flight 459. 175
Chapter 12—The Letter 177
Chapter 13—A First. 179
Chapter 14—The Real Thing. 181
Chapter 15—Think It Through .183
Chapter 16—A Different Christmas 185
Chapter 17—The Unexpected 187
Chapter 18—Difficult Assignment 189
Chapter 19—Tea Party 191
Chapter 20—Gloria's Secret 193
Chapter 21—Heart-to-Heart Talk 195
Chapter 22—Reality Check. 197
Chapter 23—Blessing in Disguise. 199
Chapter 24—Saying...*I do* 201

You Made It! (*a letter from the authors*). 203
Accepting Christ 204
Ideas for Time Spent with God 206
Need More Help? Get It! 207

Welcome to the MR. RIGHT SERIES WORKBOOK! We are so excited to have you take this journey with us! Be sure to read *Waiting for Mr. Right*, *Meeting Mr. Right*, and *Marrying Mr. Right* before starting the workbook sections for each novel. You'll get much more out of them if you already know everything that's happened with Julia and her friends.

Jesus taught people by telling them stories called parables. These parables were about typical people and events but painted a picture of spiritual truths. Julia's story is similar to a parable. It's filled with **everyday situations you can relate to**, either in your own life or in the life of someone you know.

When Jesus told a parable to a crowd, He would later talk privately with His disciples and explain the spiritual meaning behind it. That's what this workbook will do for you: it will take you aside and explain the **spiritual side** to Julia's story. You'll be able to read Bible verses about the different issues found in the novels and then think about how things are going right now **in your own life**.

This experience is between you and God, so **be honest**. Have fun as you go, knowing it's impossible to spend time with your Heavenly Father and stay the same. We are praying for you as you begin this adventure with Him. **Enjoy!**

Your sisters in Christ,

Lisa Raftery & Barbara Precourt

How to Use This Workbook

Each workbook section follows **its respective novel** chapter by chapter, analyzing the issues presented. *(Because novel 1 lays a foundation, there are multiple entries per chapter. Novels 2 & 3, however, have one single entry per chapter.)*

At the end of each workbook entry is a section called **GRAB YOUR JOURNAL.** This is your chance to write about what was just discussed. For this section, you will want to have your own journal or notebook handy.

There isn't a right or wrong way to fill out the workbook sections or write in your journal, but for those of you who may feel unsure about how to start, we've included a **sample workbook** and **sample journal** entry. This is just one way to do it, however. As you gain confidence, feel free to be creative and write in ways that express *you!*

Some of your journal entries may be short; others may be longer. One time you can write a letter. Another time simply make a list. Once in a while, you might even get poetic. It really doesn't matter as long as you're **honest and real** as you communicate with your Heavenly Father.

Okay, that's it! Read the following samples and then get started on your special journey with the One who loves you most.

Sample Workbook Entry

1 **WHEN JULIA** went away to school, she was so focused on fitting in with others, she wasn't thinking much about her relationship with God. Even so, *God was still thinking about her,* reaching out to her, and bringing people like Gary, Karen, and even Gretchen into her life to draw her back to Him.

Which character do you think God used the most to help Julia? Why?

I think God used Karen the most. She really cared about Julia and was a good friend to her. She always told the truth, even when Julia didn't want to hear it. She was a good encourager and didn't say "I told you so" all the time. She also played a big part in Julia's rescue that night at the hotel.

Psalm 139:17-18 (NLT)
[17] How precious are your thoughts about me, O God. They cannot be numbered! [18] I can't even count them; they outnumber the grains of sand...

Did you know God is thinking about you, too? In fact, He thinks more thoughts about you than the grains of sand!

Visualize an entire beach of sand. Now imagine that all those grains of sand represent thoughts that God has about you. Pretty amazing, isn't it?

Did you notice in the above verse what kind of thoughts He has concerning you? Not disappointed thoughts. Not angry or frustrated thoughts. His thoughts are *precious* ones. **God truly loves you.** How awesome that the Creator of the Universe continually has *you* on His mind!

GRAB YOUR JOURNAL and write how the above verses make you feel.

(The **GRAB YOUR JOURNAL** *response is always written in your own journal; see the next page for a sample.)*

Sample Journal Entry
(written in your own journal or notebook)

Dear Father,

I know you love me, but it's amazing that you would think about me that much! Thank you for thinking such good thoughts about me. Sometimes it's hard not to feel like you're disappointed or frustrated with me when I make mistakes. You know all the things going on in my heart. Thanks for always loving me as your daughter, even when I mess up. Thank you for forgiving me and working with me. I want to learn the lessons you're trying to teach me! I love you, Lord. Help me to think about you more and more every day.

Novel 1

Chapter 1

Unexpected Turn

1   **JULIA BEGAN** her story by sharing how restricted she felt as a Christian. She knew her parents loved her and were trying to protect her, but she still wanted to experiment with some of the things she saw other girls at school doing.

> **Proverbs 23:17-18 (NKJV)**
> [17] Do not let your heart envy sinners, but be zealous for the fear of the LORD all the day; [18] for surely there is a hereafter, and your hope will not be cut off.

*This verse instructs us not to **let** our hearts envy those who don't serve God.*

Sometimes it's a real temptation to be jealous of those who do whatever they want at the moment and seem to be having a great time!

Always remember that reckless fun only lasts for so long; then you're left to deal with the *problems or complex situations* it has brought you and everybody else along the way (ex: damaged emotions, sexually transmitted diseases, a fatal drunk driving accident, an unexpected pregnancy…)

Do you know someone who has suffered serious consequences by having *reckless fun*, maybe even yourself? What happened?

_____
_____
_____
_____
_____

Proverbs 19:23 (NLT)
Fear of the Lord leads to life, bringing security and protection from harm.

Proverbs 19:23 (CEV)
Showing respect to the LORD brings true life—if you do it, you can relax without fear of danger.

If we show respect to the LORD, trusting Him and following His directions, we'll be safer, more fulfilled, and even happier in the long run.

GRAB YOUR JOURNAL and write about any way you've been envying those who aren't serving God. Ask Him to help you see the bigger picture so you can enjoy the benefits that come from doing things His way.

2   **JULIA SAID** that part of her obsession to have a boyfriend came from spending too much time thinking about being in love. She was constantly focused on romance through books and movies, and after a while, experiencing it became her main objective in life. In fact, her tunnel vision for having a boyfriend caused her to make a lot of decisions she later regretted. What can we learn from Julia?

*Whatever we dwell on **will** eventually affect our behavior.*

> **Romans 12:2 (NLT)**
> Don't copy the behavior and customs of this world, but let God transform you into a new person by changing the way you think. Then you will learn to know God's will for you, which is good and pleasing and perfect.

> **Philippians 4:8 (NLT)**
> And now, dear brothers and sisters, one final thing. Fix your thoughts on what is true, and honorable, and right, and pure, and lovely, and admirable. Think about things that are excellent and worthy of praise.

*What are you filling **your** mind with these days?*

Honestly consider what you put into your thoughts most of the time. Take a minute and make a list of everything that comes to mind. (For example: great books, romantic novels, scary movies, gossip on the Internet, fashion magazines, good TV programs, not-so-good TV programs, great music lyrics, not-so-great music lyrics, etc.)

I fill my mind with…

_____
_____
_____
_____
_____

Now, read through that list and ask yourself: Are these things helping me to keep my focus on God and His plan for my life, or are they really more of a distraction? Write a brief answer for each thing you listed above:

GRAB YOUR JOURNAL and think about your thought life. Write to God about the things you've been focusing on lately. If you've been focusing on things that aren't the best, choose to *change what you're doing*. Ask the Lord to help you guard your mind and fill it with good, positive things—things that will help you make decisions *you can feel good about later.*

3 **THE SORORITY** invitation that Julia received ended up being a trap for her. What was the purpose of that trap? To separate her from a good relationship with those who loved her (her parents and friends) and eventually get her involved with a Mr. Wrong. Julia didn't see that invitation as a trap because she was only looking at things from a natural perspective—pledging that sorority was simply an opportunity for a new experience.

Like Julia, have you ever jumped into something that looked like a great opportunity, only to regret it later? Explain.

_____

_____

_____

_____

> **1 Peter 5:8-9 (NLT)**
> ⁸Stay alert! Watch out for your great enemy, the devil. He prowls around like a roaring lion, looking for someone to devour. ⁹Stand firm against him, and be strong in your faith. Remember that your Christian brothers and sisters all over the world are going through the same kind of suffering you are.

Did you know you have an enemy?

Live in the safety that only God can provide for you!

> **Psalm 91:1-3 (NLT)**
> ¹Those who live in the shelter of the Most High will find rest in the shadow of the Almighty. ²This I declare about the Lord: He alone is my refuge, my place of safety; he is my God, and I trust him. ³For he will rescue you from every trap and protect you from deadly disease.

GRAB YOUR JOURNAL and write to the Lord about any traps that might be laid out for you. Ask Him to protect you and open your eyes at the right times so you won't be fooled by any of them.

4 **WHEN JULIA** first opened the sorority invitation, she sensed a warning in her spirit. She knew that a sorority with a reputation for partying would not be the best environment for her. Later, when Theresa talked to her about pledging, Julia again sensed the need to say *no*. She felt she should read her Bible and pray about her decision, but instead of yielding, she stubbornly resisted doing what she knew was right. Knowing the rest of the story, think of all the tears Julia would've been spared had she chosen to obey that day!

Have you ever been drawn to read your Bible or to pray about a situation but then talked yourself into doing something else instead? If so, explain the situation and why you did that. Were you sorry later?

_____
_____
_____
_____
_____
_____

> **Be encouraged. We are all tempted at times to ignore the promptings of the Lord and do what feels better or easier at the moment. When we do, we should ask for God's forgiveness and His grace to choose better the next time.**

Galatians 5:25 (NLT)
Since we are living by the Spirit, let us follow the Spirit's leading in every part of our lives.

Following the leading of the Holy Spirit is not a one-time choice. It's a moment-by-moment decision.

GRAB YOUR JOURNAL and write about your willingness to follow the Holy Spirit's leading in *every* part of your life. Write down any areas where you know you're being stubborn right now. Ask Him to help you yield to Him in those areas, knowing that *His promptings and instructions are always for your good*—whether to guide you, protect you, or simply cause you to grow.

5   **JULIA ADMITTED** she should have discussed joining the sorority with her friends in the Bible study group. Yet she didn't. She was afraid they might confirm her initial reaction to say *no*, and truthfully, she didn't want to hear it. So in the end, Julia didn't discuss the invitation with anyone. She simply made the decision by herself.

> **Proverbs 11:14 (NKJV)**
> Where there is no counsel, the people fall; but in the multitude of counselors there is safety.

How many times do we make decisions on our own because we don't want to hear objections from others?

The above verse says that there is safety in getting godly input. Are you open to searching out good advice before making important decisions? If someone showed you a Bible verse that clearly warned you against doing something you really wanted to do, how would it affect your final decision?

_____

_____

_____

_____

_____

_____

_____

_____

_____

_____

GRAB YOUR JOURNAL and write about your willingness to listen to godly wisdom. If you need to, ask God to help you receive good advice from others and from the Bible. Also, ask Him to place friends, family, and others in your life who will love you enough to tell you the truth—*even when you don't really want to hear it!*

6 **CONVINCED HER** parents would say *no* if she asked for permission to join a sorority, Julia pledged without telling them. Once she was accepted, she worked out a plan with her dorm roommate to keep her move to the sorority house a secret from her family. She took advantage of her parents' trust in her and simply *did what she wanted*. She rationalized that lying to them was all right because it would all work out eventually. In her mind, this was the chance she needed to prove to them that she could still live for Christ *her way*.

> **How often do we do something that we know God doesn't approve of because we think we can get away with it?**

We may justify doing something wrong because we *really want to* at the moment. We convince ourselves that God understands why we're doing it, that somehow everything will *turn out all right in the end*. But does it? Have you or someone you know ever done this? Without naming names, what happened?

_____

_____

> **Proverbs 14:12 (NLT)**
> There is a path before each person that seems right, but it ends in death.
>
> **Psalm 19:13 (NLT)**
> Keep your servant from deliberate sins! Don't let them control me. Then I will be free of guilt and innocent of great sin.

No matter how justifiable wrong actions may seem at the time, they only lead to death (meaning things without the life of God—problems, negative situations, and even physical death if the situation is serious enough!)

The Psalmist asks God to keep him from committing *deliberate* sins. He was referring to purposely doing things that you know are wrong, things that clearly overstep the boundaries that God has set up in the Bible.

GRAB YOUR JOURNAL and write about what the verses in this entry mean to you. Ask God to keep you from deliberate sins and in the safety of doing what you know is right from God's Word.

Chapter 2

Mr. Wonderful

1   **WHEN JULIA** attended her first frat party, she was exposed to the unrestrained drinking her parents had warned her about before coming to college. At some point, you will have to make a decision about where *you* stand with the issue of drinking alcohol. Actually, the Bible offers many Scriptures regarding it:

> **Proverbs 23:29-35 (CEV)**
> [29]Who is always in trouble? Who argues and fights? Who has cuts and bruises? Whose eyes are red? [30]Everyone who stays up late, having just one more drink. [31]Don't even look at that colorful stuff bubbling up in the glass! It goes down so easily, [32]but later it bites like a poisonous snake. [33]You will see weird things, and your mind will play tricks on you. [34]You will feel tossed about like someone trying to sleep on a ship in a storm. [35]You will be bruised all over, without even remembering how it all happened. And you will lie awake asking, "When will morning come, so I can drink some more?"

> **Ephesians 5:17-18 (NLT)**
> [17]Don't act thoughtlessly, but understand what the Lord wants you to do. [18]Don't be drunk with wine, because that will ruin your life. Instead, be filled with the Holy Spirit...

Here we are told not to get drunk. We are also warned about some of the serious consequences of drinking too much alcohol.

> State laws prohibit the use of alcohol by minors, so if you are underage, the decision is already made for you. *You should obey the law and not drink.* Period. But as you know, there are teenagers who break the law and drink anyway, hoping they won't be caught. You may have already felt the pressure to do so. It's important you think through the consequences of drinking at your age, *beyond the obvious legal ones.*

Answer the Following Questions

Why would I want to drink alcohol?
_____
_____
_____
_____

Would I be able to drink without ever crossing the line and getting drunk?
_____
_____
_____
_____

Do I want to risk getting addicted to alcohol?
_____
_____
_____
_____

Am I willing to accept the consequences if I hurt myself or someone else because of drinking?
_____
_____
_____
_____

> In Scripture, God tells us not to get drunk. Since *He always instructs us for our own good*, why would He tell us that? When you're drunk, you are no longer completely in control, and it's harder to respond to the Holy Spirit and make wise choices. Something else is influencing your reasoning and actions. Many times unplanned premarital sex, date rape, car accidents, fights, and drug experimentation happen because someone has lost control due to alcohol. *The risks are real and very serious.*

We also cannot ignore the fact that alcohol is an addictive substance. For a lot of people, instead of turning to God, their bodies and minds turn to another drink for relaxation and relief. For some, social drinking eventually turns into a lifetime battle with alcoholism. Have you ever seen someone who was drunk or known someone with an alcohol addiction? Without naming names, explain the situation.

_____

_____

_____

> **Remember, no one *plans* to become an alcoholic! Are you willing to have something possibly control your life that much?**

Drinking is not only something you are not legally allowed to do right now, it's something you can easily live without right now! Take a moment and think about what you want your life to look like today and in the future. Then decide whether you're willing to accept the risks that alcohol brings into the picture. *A life without drinking during these years is the safer path toward seeing your dreams realized.*

The same things could be said about taking drugs to experience a high or a temporary escape from problems. The Bible doesn't talk specifically about the addictive power of drugs, but the principles and dangers associated with them are identical to the excessive use of alcohol. Both substances have the real potential to ruin your health, hurt others, or end your life prematurely.

GRAB YOUR JOURNAL and review your answers on the previous page. Has your thinking changed at all? Write to God about this subject. Ask Him to give you His wisdom in this important area.

2   **THE NIGHT** Julia found Gretchen crying in her room, Gretchen blurted out some very personal details about her life (that she was sexually active and had gotten an abortion the previous year). Did you notice Julia never repeated what Gretchen said that night? Take a minute and think about what *you* would have done with such juicy information! Would you have kept it to yourself like Julia, or would you have at least shared it with your best friend after swearing her to secrecy?

Proverbs 11:13 (NLT)
A gossip goes around telling secrets, but those who are trustworthy can keep a confidence.

As women of Christ, we don't want to be gossips! We want to be women who can be confidently trusted.

Searching within…
When someone shares her heart with you, are you faithful to keep it confidential? If you hear something about someone else, are you willing to think the best, pray for him or her, and seal your lips? Or do you take it upon yourself to spread around what you've heard?

There may be times, of course, when someone shares something so serious, you can't keep it confidential. Maybe a friend is using drugs or fighting an eating disorder. *Serious issues like those must be dealt with promptly.* In those cases, you need to break the confidence and make someone like a parent, teacher, or church leader aware of the situation. Although it's admirable to keep a secret, you're a truer friend to get help for that person—help that might even save his or her life! With this workbook entry, however, we're talking about sharing confidential information *simply because you like repeating what you know about others.*

GRAB YOUR JOURNAL and write about your ability to keep a confidence. Take this opportunity to forgive those who have betrayed your trust. If you need to, ask God to forgive you for having loose lips and a lack of self-control regarding gossip. Ask Him to create a faithful spirit in you so you can be a blessing to those around you. Remember, *you always have God to talk to* when you're just bursting to tell someone!

3   WHEN JULIA wouldn't go out with J.R.'s roommate, Fran didn't understand what the problem was. She knew that Julia wanted a Christian boyfriend, but this was just *one date*. She wasn't expecting Julia to marry this guy!

What Fran failed to recognize is that marriage doesn't usually come from out of nowhere; it *almost always* comes out of an existing relationship. We don't see many arranged marriages in our culture nowadays, so realistically, any man you date could potentially become your husband.

What do you think *you* would have said to Fran about going out with J.R.'s roommate? Would you have said *yes* or *no*? Why?

_____

_____

_____

Proverbs 9:12 (NLT)
If you become wise, you will be the one to benefit. If you scorn wisdom, you will be the one to suffer.

You must be very selective regarding whom you date.

Good Advice
If you never date a non-Christian, you won't put yourself in the position to marry one. In the same way, if you choose to only date a man who loves the Lord and is sincerely serving Him, you'll end up marrying that kind of man.
Sad Truth
Too many girls have compromised that standard for the thrill of having a boyfriend. A girl may rationalize having a non-Christian boyfriend just *for a season;* she doesn't plan on actually marrying him. Yet feelings and attachments develop in relationships, and often the girl will find herself *emotionally unable to walk away*. She eventually marries that boyfriend, hoping that everything will somehow work out. But many times it doesn't. Not only does her husband continue to have no interest in God, but her time spent in compromise has caused her to drift pretty far from her original relationship with the Lord as well. All of this could have been avoided by sticking to one simple principle: **only date a committed Christian.**

Can you see why it is so important to date only a committed Christian? It's critical that you make up your mind now, *before* an unwise but tempting offer comes along. What were your views on this subject before reading this section? Have they changed?

_____
_____
_____
_____
_____

How firm is *your* determination to only date a committed Christian? Do you think your friends would agree or disagree? Why?

_____
_____
_____
_____
_____

> **Psalm 16: 7-8 (NLT)**
> **7**I will bless the Lord who guides me; even at night my heart instructs me. **8**I know the Lord is always with me. I will not be shaken, for he is right beside me.

*Remember that **God is always right beside you**. If you ask, He'll give you the strength you need.*

GRAB YOUR JOURNAL and write about your commitment to stay strong regarding dating relationships, to remain pure and wait for God to bring the right man into your life. It may not always be easy, but you will be happy that you did in the years to come!

*(**NOTE**: "Date" is a word that has different meanings to different people. Whether you prefer to use the word "date" or "court," when we use "date" in this workbook, we're talking about spending time with someone with marriage as the eventual goal.)*

4 **JULIA SAID** it was awkward at first when she recommitted to her Thursday Bible study group. Although her friends seemed happy she was coming again, she felt uncomfortable because they knew she had moved into her sorority house.

Have you ever felt awkward around your friends after doing something foolish? Explain why you felt that way and how your friends treated you.

_____
_____
_____
_____
_____
_____
_____
_____
_____

Julia never actually admitted to her friends that she had made a mistake by joining that sorority. She just wanted to move on and act as though everything was back to how it was before she'd made that choice.

The Result

Because Julia refused to make herself accountable to anyone, still doing what she thought was best and handling things on her own, she continued to make foolish choices for the rest of the semester.

James 5:16 (NLT)

Confess your sins to each other and pray for each other so that you may be healed. The earnest prayer of a righteous person has great power and produces wonderful results.

This verse instructs us to confess our mistakes to others so they can pray for our healing.

> ### Things could have been different.
>
> Had Julia confessed her mistakes to her friends at the group, or at least to the leader, Gary, she could have begun the healing process, receiving help and support to make better choices from that point on.

Since exposing a hidden sin or area of weakness can bring support and healing, why do you think so many people are unwilling to ask for help when they desperately need it?

_____
_____
_____
_____
_____
_____
_____
_____
_____

> ### Get help!
>
> As long as you keep hurts, mistakes, or problems concealed, they will continue to grow and fester. But when you expose them to the light by sharing them with someone, they lose much of their power over you.

GRAB YOUR JOURNAL and write about how comfortable you are with confessing your faults to others. Ask the Lord to help you to be humble before others so you can always receive the freedom and healing you need. If you need to confess something, start with this journal entry to God and then show it to an adult you trust.

5 IN JULIA'S very first conversation with Jay, she explained to him she would only date Christians. That amused Jay because he *did* consider himself to be a nice Christian guy. (After all, he wasn't an atheist, right? And he had gone to church with his parents when he was younger.)

When Jay asked Julia why she thought he *wasn't* a Christian, she said it was because he was in a frat. Again that made no sense to him. How could she preach to him about being in a fraternity when she was part of a sorority (with a wild reputation)? Naturally, Jay pointed that out and then assured Julia he *was* a Christian, that there was no reason why they couldn't see each other.

Do you think it's enough for a guy to simply tell you he's a Christian? At the time, did you believe Jay was telling the truth? Explain your answers.

_____
_____
_____
_____
_____
_____
_____
_____
_____

Question	Answer
What's one of the problems with compromising godly standards?	When you stray from doing what is right, you damage your witness to others.
Why is my witness damaged?	People don't see that your life is any different from theirs.
What's so bad about that?	It makes it hard for them to accept what you're telling them about God.

> **Proverbs 25:26 (NLT)**
> If the godly give in to the wicked, it's like polluting a fountain or muddying a spring.

Bad choices and right living don't mix. If you try to mix them, you're left with a murky mess!

> When you're really thirsty, there's nothing better than a clear, cold glass of water. God wants our lives to be a refreshing fountain and a pure spring—for us and for those around us. When we start thinking and acting like people who don't respect God, we muddy or pollute the clear waters of our lives.

Take a few moments and consider if there are any areas of compromise in your life where things have gotten a bit cloudy. Write down your thoughts below.

_____
_____
_____
_____
_____
_____
_____
_____
_____
_____

GRAB YOUR JOURNAL and write to God about what you recorded above. Seek His forgiveness if you need to do so. Ask Him to help you make good choices so you'll be a refreshing, clear spring, able to enjoy a blessed life while effectively sharing your faith with the people around you.

Chapter 3

Failed Attempt

1 **IN THE** beginning, Jay was a perfect gentleman, giving Julia a simple kiss when they said goodnight. Once she told him how much she loved him, however, Jay became more aggressive. He continually pressed for more and more physically, beyond where Julia was comfortable. At that point, Julia explained her expectations as a virgin. She was only interested in spending time together and doing some light kissing. Although Jay apologized repeatedly for upsetting her, he still continued to overstep those boundaries each time they were together.

Has something similar ever happened to you or someone you know? Without naming names, explain.

_____
_____
_____
_____

> **What can we learn from Julia's experience?**
>
> It's wise to communicate your expectations and boundaries at the *start* of a dating relationship. Don't wait until a passionate moment to have this talk!

Even after setting the light-kissing rule, some of Julia and Jay's kissing got more passionate. Julia described a struggle going on inside of her. Explain that struggle and why Jay had such a hard time understanding Julia's desire to back up and take it slower.

_____
_____
_____

Young and inexperienced, Julia didn't understand and respect how strong a man's sexual drive is. Any man—Christian included—will have a hard time sticking to his convictions (or your boundaries) if the conditions are too intense. Were you aware of this before reading this novel, or is this a new thought for you? Elaborate.

> We typically focus on our own purity as girls (and rightly so), but it's important to not make it difficult for your boyfriend to maintain his purity. You can't expect him to kiss you for long periods of time without struggling with the temptation to experience more sexually. Remember: purity also includes our thought life.

Matthew 5:27-28 (CEV)
[27] You know the commandment which says, "Be faithful in marriage." [28] But I tell you that if you look at another woman and want her, you are already unfaithful in your thoughts.

Jesus places great importance on what we're thinking. Being faithful isn't just about what we do; it includes what we think about as well.

Some girls have unrealistic expectations of what their boyfriends should be able to handle. They get caught up in the romance of it all, but their boyfriends are dealing with some major passion issues, both physically and mentally.

If you find yourself dating someone who pressures you for sex, you need to end that relationship and trust God for a man who wants to *honor you*, respect God, and wait for the honeymoon. Getting to know the man that God has for you should be a peaceful, enjoyable experience, not a frustrating battle!

GRAB YOUR JOURNAL and write about how you feel regarding this subject.

Failed Attempt

2 JULIA CALLED her parents the day after Jay tried to rape her. What were you thinking during their phone conversation? Did you want Julia to tell the whole truth or not? Why?

_____
_____
_____
_____
_____

Although Julia was hurting and in need of her parents' comfort and support, she still didn't tell them about the incident in the car. Why? Because that meant admitting she'd moved into a sorority house and dated someone from a fraternity. So instead of telling her parents the truth and facing the consequences, Julia stubbornly continued lying to them, keeping her disobedience and pain a secret.

What do you think *you* would've done in her situation? Why?

_____
_____
_____
_____
_____
_____

> **Ephesians 6:1-3 (NLT)**
> ¹Children, obey your parents because you belong to the Lord, for this is the right thing to do. ²"Honor your father and mother." This is the first commandment with a promise: ³If you honor your father and mother, "things will go well for you, and you will have a long life on the earth."
>
> *Because this commandment is so important, God reveals the benefit if you obey: a long and successful life. What a great reward!*

> Having read the rest of the novel, think of the heartache Julia would've been spared had she honored her parents by telling them the truth on the phone that day.

Remember, no matter how long you've lived, your parents/guardians have lived *longer*. More than likely, *they have something valuable to share* concerning the issues you're facing and may be able to steer you away from more problems.

Some young people talk more to their peers about their problems than they do their parents. Why do you think this is? Do you realize your parents/mentors have life experience and wisdom to help you? Does that encourage you to go to them first?

_____

_____

_____

_____

Even if your parents/guardians aren't serving Christ, God can use them to protect you, and He will bless you for your obedience to them.

> **Note:** Honoring your parents/guardians doesn't mean submitting to abuse. If you are being abused in any way—physically, emotionally, or sexually—tell a trusted adult so you can get to safety. God wants you to have a life free from abuse!

GRAB YOUR JOURNAL and write about your relationship with your parents/guardians. If you haven't been honoring them, ask God to forgive you and start over! If they've made mistakes, choose to forgive them. Only God is the perfect Father (parent). Ask the Lord to *help you* honor your parents/guardians—especially when they make a decision you don't like and obeying is hard. As long as what they require from you is moral (God doesn't want you doing wrong things for anyone), you can submit to their leadership knowing God is pleased with you for obeying. In fact, even if their decision isn't perfect, He'll bring a blessing out of the situation. Best of all, you can have confidence that God will give you a long life in which things go well for you—not just a mediocre life, but a *great* life!

Failed Attempt

3   **JULIA SAID** she could feel her parents' love reaching out to her when she was back home during spring break. Although her mom and dad didn't realize it, their hugs and kisses were helping to heal hurts she was hiding inside.

Have you ever been the one who was hurting on the inside but wouldn't tell anyone? Did anyone help to heal your hurts without even knowing it? Explain.

_____

_____

_____

_____

_____

> **Never underestimate the impact of a smile, a kind word, or an embrace. Don't undervalue those little kindnesses.**

Galatians 5:22-23 (NLT)
²²But the Holy Spirit produces this kind of fruit in our lives: love, joy, peace, patience, kindness, goodness, faithfulness, ²³gentleness, and self-control. There is no law against these things!

Be sensitive to the Holy Spirit when dealing with others.

Be willing to reach out.

If the Holy Spirit prompts you to call or text a friend to see how she is doing, that may seem trivial to you, but to her, it could mean everything. In fact, your acts of Christ-like love may be healing wounds you cannot see!

GRAB YOUR JOURNAL and ask your Heavenly Father to make you sensitive to the needs of others. Ask Him to help you show the kindness that will bring healing to hurting hearts. If you have hurts today that others cannot see, *ask God to begin healing you*. Then tell a trusted adult so they can support you as you heal.

Chapter 4

Facing the Problem

1   **JULIA TOLD** Jay she knew he wasn't really a Christian by the way he talked when they were together. You can tell a lot about a person by what he or she says. People talk about what's important to them! In fact, many times their words reveal *what they're going through* in their lives.

During the next couple of days, pay close attention to the conversations around you. Then, without naming names, record some interesting things you learned by listening carefully to what was said:

_____
_____
_____
_____
_____
_____

> **Matthew 12:34-35 (NLT)**
> ³⁴You brood of snakes! How could evil men like you speak what is good and right? For whatever is in your heart determines what you say. ³⁵A good person produces good things from the treasury of a good heart, and an evil person produces evil things from the treasury of an evil heart.

Jesus was speaking to some religious leaders who scoffed at one of His miracles, refusing to believe that His power was from God.

> By addressing the hearts and intentions of these religious leaders, Jesus reminds all of us that our words reveal *whatever is in our hearts—* good or bad. Eventually, your true self will come out in your conversation.

Facing the Problem

The same is true of the friends you're making. If your friends' hearts are filled with good things, it will become obvious *by what they say and do.* If their hearts are filled with wrong things, over time that fact will become just as obvious!

Evaluate how *your* speech and actions are influenced by your closest friends (positively or negatively). If negatively, are you open to making better friends? Write your response below:

_____
_____
_____
_____
_____

So, what do other people know about you from what *you* say? Do they know that Jesus is the Lord of your life? Do they know where you stand on important issues? Are your conversations communicating a Christ-like attitude or a negative view of life and people? Take a few moments and think about what you've been talking about lately. What do your words reveal about what's in your heart?

_____
_____
_____
_____
_____

GRAB YOUR JOURNAL and write to the Lord about this. Ask Him to help you deal with any negative things you hear yourself saying (maybe a lack of forgiveness toward someone, a bad attitude toward a parent or teacher, or fear in areas where you haven't learned to trust Him yet). Thank the Lord for giving you a heart filled with *good treasure.* As you read your Bible and cultivate your relationships with God and others, that treasure will surely grow!

2 **WHEN JULIA** broke up with Jay, the girls in the sorority house urged her to give him another chance. They liked Jay and felt he was too handsome and charming to let go—even though they knew what had happened in the car. To them, Julia was being unreasonable not to date him anymore. Did that surprise you?

How do *you* cope when none of your peers understand your moral convictions? What do you do when no amount of explaining seems to get through to them?

_____

_____

_____

> **1 Corinthians 2:14 (NLT)**
> But people who aren't spiritual can't receive these truths from God's Spirit. It all sounds foolish to them and they can't understand it, for only those who are spiritual can understand what the Spirit means.

Keep in mind that God's ways do not make sense to people who are not spiritual.

To some, your arguments from the Bible have no validity. They can't fully understand spiritual truths until they receive Christ as their personal Savior and allow the Holy Spirit to teach and guide them.

Remember
Some people won't understand your decision to do what's right, no matter what you say to them.
You're responsible for your own choices, and God is pleased when you put Him and His Word first.
How you live your life will speak to people more than any verbal argument.
The visible blessings you receive from doing things the Lord's way will be hard for others to deny!

GRAB YOUR JOURNAL and write about a time when you were misunderstood. Be encouraged: when those times come, you aren't alone—God's right there with you!

Facing the Problem

3 **WHEN JULIA** told Karen what had happened with Jay in the car, Karen shared that the Bible study group had been worried about Julia dating Jay, praying for her for over two months. Those were some good friends!

Sometimes we see our friends going through problems we cannot fix for them. Even so, there *is* something important we can do for them: we can pray for them! *Prayer is powerful.* It can bring God into a situation that only He can fix.

Acts 12: 5-17 (CEV)
⁵While Peter was being kept in jail, the church never stopped praying to God for him. ⁶The night before Peter was to be put on trial, he was asleep and bound by two chains. A soldier was guarding him on each side, and two other soldiers were guarding the entrance to the jail. ⁷Suddenly an angel from the Lord appeared, and light flashed around in the cell. The angel poked Peter in the side and woke him up. Then he said, "Quick! Get up!" The chains fell off his hands, ⁸and the angel said, "Get dressed and put on your sandals." Peter did what he was told. Then the angel said, "Now put on your coat and follow me." ⁹Peter left with the angel, but he thought everything was only a dream. ¹⁰They went past the two groups of soldiers, and when they came to the iron gate to the city, it opened by itself. They went out and were going along the street, when all at once the angel disappeared. ¹¹Peter now realized what had happened, and he said, "I am certain that the Lord sent his angel to rescue me from Herod and from everything the Jewish leaders planned to do to me." ¹²Then Peter went to the house of Mary the mother of John whose other name was Mark. Many of the Lord's followers had come together there and were praying. ¹³Peter knocked on the gate, and a servant named Rhoda came to answer. ¹⁴When she heard Peter's voice, she was too excited to open the gate. She ran back into the house and said that Peter was standing there. ¹⁵"You are crazy!" everyone told her. But she kept saying that it was Peter. Then they said, "It must be his angel." ¹⁶But Peter kept on knocking, until finally they opened the gate. They saw him and were completely amazed. ¹⁷Peter motioned for them to keep quiet. Then he told how the Lord had led him out of jail…

> Because of the grace of God and the *continual* prayers of others, Peter experienced a supernatural escape from prison. *Prayer brings about what nothing else can.* Peter's friends couldn't break him out of jail, but they could pray for God's supernatural intervention. When they did, they got supernatural results!

Can you think of a time when the prayers of others helped get you or someone you know the supernatural help needed for a problem? Without naming names, write what happened:

_____
_____
_____
_____
_____

When a problem arises in your life, do you ask someone to pray for you? Why or why not?

_____
_____
_____
_____
_____

Can you think of someone who needs your prayers? Is his or her situation critical and in need of God's supernatural help? Are you willing to pray faithfully for that person, more than just a time or two?

GRAB YOUR JOURNAL and write a prayer for that person right now. Ask your Heavenly Father to move on his or her behalf and meet every need: spirit, soul, and body. Continue to pray in the days and weeks to come. Only God knows what miracle you may eventually see!

Chapter 5

A Brand New Deal

1   **BY NOW** Julia had talked with Jay face to face, making their breakup official. Shaken by the episode in his car, she did not want to see Jay ever again! Even so, as time progressed, she began to run into him more and more around campus and at church. After a while, Julia found herself reminiscing about the past with Jay. She had to force herself not to think about all the good times they'd shared, how much they used to laugh together. She had to admit *she missed being with him.*

Let's ask some questions.

As you read this chapter and saw Julia slipping back into a dating relationship with Jay, how did you feel about it?

☐ happy they were back together

☐ frustrated Julia had forgotten the pressure and fear she once felt with Jay

☐ like shaking Julia and reminding her Jay had tried to *rape* her!

What would you have said to Julia? Do you think she would have listened?

_____
_____
_____
_____
_____
_____

In the previous box, you may have written, *"What are you thinking, Julia?"*

> Actually, Julia *wasn't* thinking—she was feeling. How was she feeling? Very lonely. In fact, she was so lonely, her mind chose to focus on the *good things* from her past relationship with Jay, causing all the negatives to be pushed further and further into the background, *even as serious as those negatives were.*

When we've experienced a broken relationship, sometimes our minds will exaggerate how good things were from the past, making them out to be *much better than they actually were* at the time. That can cause us to keep longing for things we enjoyed in the past, fail to accurately evaluate the present, and then end up making the same mistakes again.

Since Julia began to focus only on what she wanted from the past with Jay—the good and fun parts—it caused her to hang on to a relationship that God wanted her to end permanently.

Would you be able to walk away from a handsome and charming guy like Jay if you sensed that God wanted you to? Explain your answer.

_____

_____

_____

_____

_____

_____

Philippians 3:13-14 (NLT)
¹³No, dear brothers and sisters, I have not achieved it, but I focus on this one thing: Forgetting the past and looking forward to what lies ahead, ¹⁴I press on to reach the end of the race and receive the heavenly prize for which God, through Christ Jesus, is calling us.

How do these verses apply to Julia's situation with Jay?

Theses verses aren't saying that Julia was supposed to completely forget about what had happened with Jay, living in denial. On the contrary, *she needed to remember that he was dangerous* and shift her focus from Jay to her relationship with the Lord. Julia had a lot of spiritual growing to do before God could bring her together with the great man she would someday marry.

About moving forward...
Sometimes we have to force ourselves to forget what is behind and look to what is ahead. We have to catch God's vision for our future and keep our eyes fixed on where we're going with the Lord.
It's not that we no longer remember what happened yesterday; it's that we choose to leave it behind us as we press into what God has for us today and in the future.
We must be determined *not to take even one step backward!*

The void Julia experienced after breaking up with Jay was normal. Transitioning into what we know God wants for us can be uncomfortable and even painful for a little while. However, we'll experience *a lot more pain in the long run* if we ignore the truth and refuse to walk away from a wrong relationship. Conversely, we'll experience greater happiness in the long run if we trust God for our future, doing what is right *now*.

Have you ever refused to walk away from a wrong relationship when you should have? What additional problems did it cause you?

_____

_____

_____

GRAB YOUR JOURNAL and write down your thoughts about trusting God and leaving the past behind. If you're in a time of transition that isn't easy, ask God to strengthen you and give you the resolve to *stay the course anyway!* Know that sticking to God's plan for you will always bring you more joy and fulfillment than anything the past had to offer. Ask Him to help you see things in your life clearly so you can confidently trust Him for all that He's promised both today and tomorrow.

2 **AFTER JAY** went to the altar for salvation, Karen warned Julia to keep her relationship with him strictly as friends. She felt it was too soon to tell if Jay's actions were genuine or just a ploy to get back with Julia. What good advice that turned out to be! Unfortunately, Julia didn't wait to find that out. Because she was lonely, she was too quick to believe Jay *was* a Christian now, he *had* changed, and she would be safe with him. As you know, that impatience almost cost her life!

Can you think of a time when impatience cost *you*? Explain.

_____
_____
_____
_____
_____
_____

Hebrews 6:11-12 (CEV)
¹¹We wish that each of you would always be eager to show how strong and lasting your hope really is. ¹²Then you would never be lazy. You would be following the example of those who had faith and were patient until God kept his promise to them.

*Most of us understand that we need faith to receive God's promises. Yet we often forget the **patience** part!*

In order to receive what God has promised us, we have to continue to believe *and* remain patient with His timing. That can sometimes be quite a challenge!

Hebrews 10:35-36 (NLT)
³⁵So do not throw away this confident trust in the Lord. Remember the great reward it brings you! ³⁶Patient endurance is what you need now, so that you will continue to do God's will. Then you will receive all that he has promised.

God assures us that as we confidently trust Him and continue to do His will (what He wants), we will receive all that He's promised us.

> **Remember:** Our patient endurance to keep believing and serving *will* bring us a great reward! Getting impatient, on the other hand, often causes us to make wrong decisions and *rush ahead* of God's plan for us. It allows negative situations to develop and can even postpone the blessings God has been preparing for us all along.

In Julia's case, impatience for romance caused her to go through several traumas God never intended for her to experience (two attempted rapes, a drug overdose, and the stress of hiding the truth from her parents).

Being impatient for romance is common among teen girls and singles. Why do you think this is?

_____
_____
_____
_____
_____
_____

> ### Something to think about...
> Most of Julia's heartaches could have been avoided had she chosen to endure the temporary loneliness she was feeling and continue to trust God to mature her and give her a boyfriend when He felt she was ready.

GRAB YOUR JOURNAL and consider the following: Are there any areas in your life where you've grown impatient? Have you become discouraged because what you're believing for seems to be taking too long to happen? Are you tempted to throw away your trust in the Lord and make things happen on your own? Write down your response to those questions and ask the Lord to help you keep a confident trust in Him *no matter what.* If you continue to pursue your relationship with God, believing for what He has promised and following His directions along the way, you will not be disappointed in the big picture of your life.

3　**AFTER JULIA** and Jay worked out their new deal to date again, they sealed it with a kiss outside the sorority house. When Julia walked into the lobby a few moments later, she realized that Carrie and her roommate had witnessed that kiss through the parlor window. Their teasing made that clear.

What's the lesson to be learned? *People are watching you as a Christian.* Carrie and her roommate probably wouldn't have thought too much of a little kiss like that—except for the fact that Julia was kissing Jay after insisting she'd never date him again!

Do you realize that people are watching *you?* How do you feel about that?

_____

_____

_____

> <u>**Matthew 5:14-16 (NLT)**</u>
> [14]You are the light of the world—like a city on a hilltop that cannot be hidden. [15]No one lights a lamp and then puts it under a basket. Instead, a lamp is placed on a stand, where it gives light to everyone in the house. [16]In the same way, let your good deeds shine out for all to see, so that everyone will praise your heavenly Father.

Doesn't it feel good to know that God wants *you* to be His light in this world? He loves you and is proud of who you are becoming in Christ. He wants to use each of us as His representatives. That is the highest compliment we could ever receive! It's not so much about us being perfect in front of others. That's too much to ask of us before heaven. Instead, it's about us having a *vibrant and real* relationship with our Heavenly Father, one that changes our character and lives for the better.

> Being a Christian is about getting to know God better and better, learning His ways, and living our lives to please Him. It's about asking for forgiveness when we make mistakes and pressing on to learn, grow, and live this life God's given us to the fullest. (This is not just for us, but also *to help others.*)

When people see you having an honest relationship with God, one that helps you deal with both positive and negative situations, they will be drawn to that type of light. So take a moment and think about how your walk with God is *shining out for all to see*. What exactly *are* people seeing?

Write down some of the good things people see you do.

Write down areas you know aren't bringing praise to the Lord.

Now write down some ways you can improve.
We all have something we can do better! God is willing to help us change; all we have to do is ask.

GRAB YOUR JOURNAL and write to the Lord about what is already shining bright before others (and what needs to shine brighter).

Chapter 6

Awakened Desire

1 **BEING BACK** together with Jay meant finally going to her first dance, and Julia was thrilled! She was going with a handsome guy all the girls admired, and her sorority sisters were showering her with attention, providing everything she needed for her dream night. Deep down, Julia knew it was a mistake to date Jay again, but she didn't care at the moment. She was having a great time, and all was going her way—*or so she thought*. What unforeseen problems were actually on the horizon?

_____

_____

_____

The Truth
When we make a bad decision, the negative consequences are not always immediate, lulling us into a false sense of security. But we can be sure that whenever we choose to do what isn't right, a storm begins to brew and head in our direction. (Not because God wants it that way, but simply because there are always consequences for our choices in life, good or bad.)

<u>Galatians 6:7-8 (CEV)</u>
⁷You cannot fool God, so don't make a fool of yourself! You will harvest what you plant. ⁸If you follow your selfish desires, you will harvest destruction, but if you follow the Spirit, you will harvest eternal life.

*The choices you're making **now** shape your future.*

GRAB YOUR JOURNAL and ask the Lord if there's a storm coming your way because of making wrong choices. If He reminds you of something, ask Him to forgive you, to have mercy on you, and to give you His grace to get you through that storm. If you aren't aware of anything, write out a prayer asking the Lord to give you a daily weather report on your activities. Ask Him to help you plant good things in your life *now* so that you can reap a good harvest later!

2   **When Julia** agreed to date Jay again, she conveniently "forgot" to mention it to Karen. In fact, she never did tell her; Karen figured it out herself when she saw Julia and Jay holding hands together at church.

The results
How did Julia respond once she realized Karen knew she and Jay were dating again?
How was Julia's relationship with Karen affected?

What should you do when you see a friend like Julia making a foolish or potentially dangerous mistake? Should you close your eyes and ears to what's happening, or should you talk to her?

_____
_____
_____
_____

> **Proverbs 27:6 (NLT)**
> Wounds from a sincere friend are better than many kisses from an enemy.

Being a sincere friend means encouraging those you care about to do what is right.

Although honest words may hurt at first, this verse in Proverbs says that wounds from a true friend are better than kisses from someone who doesn't really care.

A true friend will love you enough to be honest, *even if it upsets you.* Their motive is more about *helping you* than protecting themselves. A false friend will merely tell you what you want to hear in order to keep you happy with them.

Would you rather have a friend who's honest or one who simply tells you what you want to hear? Explain your answer.

_____
_____
_____
_____
_____

Being a good friend isn't always easy. Sometimes it's hard to do the right thing, especially if your friend gets mad at you for being honest. Eventually, she may come back and thank you for loving her enough to tell the truth. Then again, she may never appreciate what you tried to do. Regardless, God will reward you for trying to help your friend the best you could.

GRAB YOUR JOURNAL and write about any friends you need to forgive for hurting you when you tried to help them. Have you ever hurt a friend trying to help you? Is there anyone you need to ask forgiveness from as well? Ask the Lord to help you grow in the area of friendships, to cause you to be a genuine friend to others and to keep you from turning against those who are trying to be a good friend to you.

Awakened Desire

3 **AT THE** end of this chapter, Julia acknowledged it was a mistake to date Jay again, but she didn't want to give him up quite yet. She sensed the danger and still went on anyway. Why?

> Julia's motives at this point were very selfish. She wasn't thinking of Jay's feelings or how this relationship would eventually affect him. Being with Jay kept her from being lonely, and that was her main concern. She simply chose to ignore the long-term so she could enjoy the moment *her way*.

> **Proverbs 22:3 (NLT)**
> A prudent person foresees danger and takes precautions. The simpleton goes blindly on and suffers the consequences.

Do not ignore warning signs in any relationship!

Julia ignored the warning signs with Jay and ended up suffering emotional and physical consequences. (The physical consequence being the drug overdose.)

> **Consider this...**
> Other people will suffer consequences right along with us when we choose to ignore God's warnings.

In this novel, we saw Julia's choices affect other people as well. Jay suffered deeply hurt feelings when he realized Julia really wasn't committed to their relationship past graduation. Julia's friends had to endure the stress and inconvenience of the rescue and hospital watch. Julia's parents had to fly to their unconscious daughter's side in a hospital room, not knowing if she would live or die. While there was forgiveness for Julia in all of this (as there is for all of us when we blow it), how much better to exercise more wisdom in the first place!

GRAB YOUR JOURNAL and write about this verse in Proverbs. What does it mean to you? Ask God to help you take precautions when you see danger ahead. Invite Him to develop you into a wise woman—one who closely follows His Word and His ways in order to avoid unnecessary problems for you and others.

Chapter 7

Warnings

1 **WHEN GRETCHEN** talked with Julia, she was relieved to hear Julia didn't visit Jay's room at his frat house. Many times girls sent off to college are warned not to go to a guy's room or apartment alone. Often when a girl is given a rule like that, she'll initially agree with it, inwardly committing to follow it. *Yeah, that's good advice. I'll be careful not to do that.*

Yet later, when she's interested in spending time with a guy, she'll make an exception. *I know I said I wouldn't do this, but with Josh it's different. He'd never do anything to hurt me.* Trustingly, she goes alone to his apartment and disregards the wise advice that made so much sense to her at an earlier time.

If nothing negative happens that first time, she begins to feel confident in her ability to judge a guy's character and intentions. She makes that exception more and more until her commitment to take precautions *simply fades away.*

The problem with compromising wise principles
You gradually let your guard down, potentially opening the door to someone that *will* harm you.
You may find yourself in unprotected places with someone that you *think* is safe but really isn't.

Something to think about…
No one gets ready for a date *planning* to be raped later on in the evening! It only takes one time alone with the wrong person to experience something truly painful.

Many girls are talked into going places where their safety is at risk. Why do you think that happens?

_____

_____

_____

Warnings

It's not wrong to be a trusting person, but when it comes to safety and protection, we must be diligent to *think ahead* and make the wisest choices possible.

I Peter 5:8 (NKJV)
Be sober, be vigilant; because your adversary the devil walks about like a roaring lion, seeking whom he may devour.

Proverbs 2:11 (NLT)
Wise choices will watch over you. Understanding will keep you safe.

Here we are warned to be serious, rational, and alert to trouble. Why? So we won't be harmed.

It's a good idea to brainstorm simple rules to keep you from getting into compromising or dangerous situations. Some examples are given below; add a few of your own:

I will…	I will not…
try to keep my cell phone charged in case of emergency.	get into any car whose driver has been drinking.
always be honest about the people I spend time with at school, in my free time, and online.	meet secretly with anyone, especially someone I've met through a friend or online.
make sure I have enough cash with me in case I need to get home on my own.	go to parties my parents / guardians don't know about.
_____	_____
_____	_____

GRAB YOUR JOURNAL and write about your commitment to protect yourself. Ask God to grant you wisdom in each scenario you face—to keep you from making repeated exceptions that break down your resolve to stick to the rules (*rules that could end up saving your life*).

2 **AS GRETCHEN** talked with Julia, she explained how she had come to college as a virgin, that she had intended to stay that way. As we know from reading the rest of her story, things did not work out as she anticipated. While Gretchen had *good intentions* to remain a virgin, she didn't have a *plan* to accomplish her goal. She had a general end result she was hoping for, but no guidelines to direct and protect her along that desired path.

Do you think most people have a plan to accomplish their goals in life? Why or why not?

_____

_____

What can you learn from Gretchen?
To accomplish your goals in life—whatever they may be—you must be *intentional*.
As opportunities and decisions come up, you need to thoughtfully consider how each choice will affect achieving your goals.
It's good to ask yourself, *"Will doing this bring me closer to my objectives, or will it distract me and draw me away?"*
A few illustrations
If your goal is to graduate college, you have to carefully consider how you spend your time. If you are socializing much more than studying, you're probably *not* going to do well. You must be intentional about how you manage your time. Done right, you can have time for both work and fun. They simply need to be in proper balance.
Is your goal to be a virgin—or a spiritually-restored virgin*—until your wedding night? Then have a plan to get there! If you choose to date, be particular about whom you date. Only date a Christian man who wants to wait, too. Express your expectations and boundaries *up front*. Pray for renewed strength and vision to wait. Read Scriptures that reinforce your commitment to do things according to God's perfect will. Ask God to make your desire to have a beautiful and pure honeymoon stronger than your desire to have a fleeting moment of fun. Guard against isolated time alone with your boyfriend. If you sense a tempting moment coming, *run!*   **See last journal entry in Chapter 11*

Warnings

If you're simply *hoping* to reach your goals, you probably won't. You need to set up and *stick to* planned out guidelines regarding what you want to achieve.

> **2 Thessalonians 1:11b (CEV)**
> We pray for God's power to help you do all the good things that you hope to do and that your faith makes you want to do.

*With wise planning and God's help, you **will** make it to the finish line!*

Take a few moments and list some goals for your life—big and small.

Personal Goals	Spiritual Goals

GRAB YOUR JOURNAL and write about the goals you listed above. Ask the Lord to help you to be *purposeful* regarding those goals, to give you the *right strategies* along the way to see them achieved. If you choose to diligently guard your dreams, with God's power, you will see them accomplished!

3   **GRETCHEN TEARFULLY** shared with Julia that her boyfriend, Brad, had raped her at his fraternity house. She described how he had tricked her into going to his room and how he had taken advantage of her trust in him. She relayed his spiteful words to her when she awoke later and how he stayed in bed and made her walk back to her dorm alone. Unfortunately, *this tragedy is nothing new.* Read the story of Tamar below:

---

2 Samuel 13:1-20 (NLT)

[1] Now David's son Absalom had a beautiful sister named Tamar. And Amnon, her half brother, fell desperately in love with her. [2] Amnon became so obsessed with Tamar that he became ill. She was a virgin, and Amnon thought he could never have her. [3] But Amnon had a very crafty friend—his cousin Jonadab. He was the son of David's brother Shimea. [4] One day Jonadab said to Amnon, "What's the trouble? Why should the son of a king look so dejected morning after morning?" So Amnon told him, "I am in love with Tamar, my brother Absalom's sister." [5] "Well," Jonadab said, "I'll tell you what to do. Go back to bed and pretend you are ill. When your father comes to see you, ask him to let Tamar come and prepare some food for you. Tell him you'll feel better if she prepares it as you watch and feeds you with her own hands." [6] So Amnon lay down and pretended to be sick. And when the king came to see him, Amnon asked him, "Please let my sister Tamar come and cook my favorite dish as I watch. Then I can eat it from her own hands." [7] So David agreed and sent Tamar to Amnon's house to prepare some food for him. [8] When Tamar arrived at Amnon's house, she went to the place where he was lying down so he could watch her mix some dough. Then she baked his favorite dish for him. [9] But when she set the serving tray before him, he refused to eat. "Everyone get out of here," Amnon told his servants. So they all left. [10] Then he said to Tamar, "Now bring the food into my bedroom and feed it to me here." So Tamar took his favorite dish to him. [11] But as she was feeding him, he grabbed her and demanded, "Come to bed with me, my darling sister." [12] "No, my brother!" she cried. "Don't be foolish! Don't do this to me! Such wicked things aren't done in Israel. [13] Where could I go in my shame? And you would be called one of the greatest fools in Israel. Please, just speak to the king about it, and he will let you marry me." [14] But Amnon wouldn't listen to her, and since he was stronger than she was, he raped her. [15] Then suddenly Amnon's love turned to hate, and he hated her even more than he had loved her. "Get out of here!" he snarled at her. [16] "No, no!" Tamar cried. "Sending me away now is worse than what you've already done to me." But Amnon wouldn't listen to her. [17] He shouted for his servant and demanded, "Throw this woman out, and lock the door behind her!" [18] So the servant put her out and locked the door behind her. She was wearing a long, beautiful robe, as was the custom in those days for the king's virgin daughters. [19] But now Tamar tore her robe and put ashes on her head. And then, with her face in her hands, she went away crying. [20] Her brother Absalom saw her and asked, "Is it true that Amnon has been with you? Well, my sister, keep quiet for now, since he's your brother. Don't you worry about it." So Tamar lived as a desolate woman in her brother Absalom's house.

As you read through these verses, did you notice similarities in Tamar and Gretchen's stories? What were they?

_____
_____
_____
_____
_____

> Oftentimes, a girl will feel as if she's the only one to have gone through a certain situation when, in reality, many other women have experienced the very same thing.

Of all the distressing emotions both Gretchen and Tamar had to face after their traumatic experiences, perhaps the most difficult one was that of *shame*.

> According to **Wordsmyth.net**, shame is: *emotional pain brought about by the knowledge that one has done something wrong, embarrassing, or disgraceful.*
>
> **Infoplease.com** says shame is: *painful feeling arising from the consciousness of something dishonorable, improper, ridiculous, etc.* **done by oneself or another.**

It was shame that caused Gretchen to continue dating Brad despite the horrible thing he had done to her. Shame caused Tamar to tear her virgin robe, run away with her face covered, and live in her brother's house, devastated.

> Notice that a feeling of shame can come upon a person involved in a negative situation *whether or not she chose to be a part of it.* Gretchen and Tamar didn't want to have sex with those men, yet they still felt an overwhelming shame after they were raped. *Because shame is attached to the wrong action,* those who have experienced it—willingly or not—often have to deal with the shameful feelings that accompany the experience.

> God intended for sexual intimacy to be experienced in a loving marriage relationship. When it's not, the dynamics change.

Unfortunately, girls who have been raped, molested, or seduced, may feel a great amount of shame afterwards, causing them to keep the pain of what happened hidden from others.

You may be reading this section battling your own feelings of shame for things that have happened in your past. Some of the shame you're feeling may have been caused by wrong decisions you made. Or maybe you're fighting shameful feelings because of something someone else did to you.

> **Hebrews 12:2 (NKJV)**
> …looking unto Jesus, the author and finisher of our faith, who for the joy that was set before Him endured the cross, despising the shame, and has sat down at the right hand of the throne of God.

Because Jesus experienced great shame, He can fully understand what you may be feeling.

The writer of Hebrews refers to the shame Christ endured on the cross. Remember, in Jesus' culture, being crucified was a very shameful and dishonorable way to die. He had to hang on that cross stripped virtually naked, with all eyes watching. He had to endure insults, mocking, and the humiliation of dying a convicted criminal's death, even though He was the innocent Son of God.

Why does that verse say He endured the shame of the cross? It says He did it *"for the joy that was set before Him."* What was that joy? It was knowing He was saving you from sin (and all its effects—including shame) and making it possible for you to have fellowship with God once again.

How does what we've shared so far affect your view of *shame*? Did you realize that Jesus Himself knew shame?

_____
_____
_____
_____

*Think of it! Jesus loved and valued you so much that He chose to bear your shame on the cross so you could accept what He did for you and live **totally free**.*

Ephesians 1:4-7 (NLT)
⁴Even before he made the world, God loved us and chose us in Christ to be holy and without fault in his eyes. ⁵God decided in advance to adopt us into his own family by bringing us to himself through Jesus Christ. This is what he wanted to do, and it gave him great pleasure. ⁶So we praise God for the glorious grace he has poured out on us who belong to his dear Son. ⁷He is so rich in kindness and grace that he purchased our freedom with the blood of his Son and forgave our sins.

Remember Gretchen? She willingly came to Jesus and left her shame at the foot of the cross, where it could no longer torment her. Because she was cleansed and free from what Brad did to her and from her own poor choices, she was able to start a new life.

Psalm 34:5 (NLT)
Those who look to him for help will be radiant with joy; no shadow of shame will darken their faces.

Today you can look to the Lord and be radiant with joy as He removes any shadow of shame from your life.

GRAB YOUR JOURNAL and write to the Lord, bringing Him any shame you feel. Ask for His forgiveness for anything you may have done. Release forgiveness toward anyone who has hurt you. (It may not be easy, but forgiveness is an important key to healing and freedom. If you need help forgiving, ask an adult you trust to help walk you through the process.) Refuse to hold on to shame. Know that as you leave it at the cross, you can walk away—free to experience God's very best!

4 **WHEN JULIA** finally met her friend at The Coffee Cup, what did you think of Karen confronting Julia about dating Jay again? Did you see Karen as being a good friend, or did you think she was meddling in something that was none of her business?

_____
_____
_____
_____
_____

Review the conversation Karen had with Julia in the middle of Chapter 7. She was firm but kind, asking questions and trying to make Julia understand why dating Jay again was a big mistake. She didn't talk arrogantly, as if *she* would never do what Julia was doing. Instead, out of love for her friend, she spoke humbly and honestly from the conviction of her heart. She had the courage to tell Julia the truth *even though she knew her friend really didn't want to hear it.*

Would you be afraid to warn a friend if you saw her making a mistake that could eventually cause her harm? Explain your answer.

_____
_____
_____
_____
_____
_____

> **Proverbs 28:23 (NLT)**
> In the end, people appreciate honest criticism far more than flattery.

Our friends will appreciate us more when we share the truth (rather than simply telling them what they want to hear.)

Warnings

As we discussed in an earlier entry, a good friend will speak out the truth in love. But what does that mean?

Here we're instructed to gently guide a straying friend back onto the right path. That means that our words need to be kind and encouraging, not harsh and condemning.

> **Galatians 6:1-2 (NKJV)**
> ¹Brethren, if a man is overtaken in any trespass, you who are spiritual restore such a one in a spirit of gentleness, considering yourself lest you also be tempted. ²Bear one another's burdens, and so fulfill the law of Christ.

What do the above verses say about maintaining a gentle attitude when correcting someone?

_____

_____

_____

_____

> If we speak to someone in an arrogant way (as if *we* would never do such a thing), we may one day find ourselves tempted to make the very same mistake!

> **Proverbs 16:18 (NLT)**
> Pride goes before destruction, and haughtiness before a fall.

Being prideful and arrogant sets us up to fail.

Think about how you deal with friends when they are making wrong choices and need help getting back on the right path. It's best to approach them with sincere concern and a humble heart, using firm but kind words. They'll be more likely to listen to you *if they feel you really care* about what they are going through.

GRAB YOUR JOURNAL and write about the verses you've just read. Ask the Lord to train you to be the kind of friend who has the courage to confront when necessary—but in a kind way.

Chapter 8

Living the Lie

1 **IN THIS** chapter, we saw Julia living two separate lives. On one hand, she was trying to live as a Christian. She was going to church, attending a Bible study, and reaching out to Gretchen with the truth of God's love. At the same time, she was continuing to deceive her parents, lying to them about where she was living and assuring them that everything at college was just fine—no mention of sorority life, Jay, or the upcoming dance. One moment she was using her mouth to speak the truth to Gretchen, the next to tell lies to her parents.

Even though Julia was getting some of the things she wanted by lying, was she at peace with herself while living the lie? Explain.

_____
_____
_____
_____

What were *you* feeling as Julia continued to deceive her parents about her life at college? Did you approve or disapprove? Were you nervous she would get caught? Did you wish she'd tell them the truth?

_____
_____
_____
_____
_____
_____

> Take a moment to think about what comes out of *your* mouth. Like Julia, are both blessing and cursing coming from your lips? Truth *and* lies? Encouragement *and* discouragement? Are your conversations fresh, bitter, or a combination of both?

> **James 3:9-13 (NLT)**
> ⁹Sometimes it praises our Lord and Father, and sometimes it curses those who have been made in the image of God. ¹⁰And so blessing and cursing come pouring out of the same mouth. Surely, my brothers and sisters, this is not right! ¹¹Does a spring of water bubble out with both fresh water and bitter water? ¹²Does a fig tree produce olives, or a grapevine produce figs? No, and you can't draw fresh water from a salty spring. ¹³If you are wise and understand God's ways, prove it by living an honorable life, doing good works with the humility that comes from wisdom.
>
> **James 3:2 (NLT)**
> Indeed, we all make many mistakes. For if we could control our tongues, we would be perfect and could also control ourselves in every other way.

Julia repeatedly struggled with self-control when it came to getting involved in sorority life and a relationship with Jay. If she had brought her tongue under control, speaking the truth to her parents and friends at all times, how might things have gone differently?

_____
_____
_____
_____
_____
_____

GRAB YOUR JOURNAL and write how the above verses relate to your life. Ask the Father to help you control your tongue so you can live an honorable life and gain self-control in other ways.

2 **AS JULIA** exchanged small talk with Gretchen on the way to the Bible study, she reflected on her initial impression of her. At first, Gretchen had seemed confident and happy (like she had it all together). Yet as Julia got to know her, she realized Gretchen was actually hurt, insecure, and miserable on the inside. Without naming names, have you ever known anyone like Gretchen? Explain.

_____

_____

> **1 Samuel 16:7b (NLT)**
> "...The Lord doesn't see things the way you see them. People judge by outward appearance, but the Lord looks at the heart."

Often we let ourselves be influenced and intimidated by what we see on the outside. But only God knows what's really going on in a person's heart.

Do you find it intimidating to share Christ with people who don't seem to want or even need Him in their lives?
Some things to consider
People *do* need Christ in their lives, even if they don't think so!
We don't always know *why* a person seems indifferent to the Lord.
A person may be putting up a bold front against God while yearning on the inside to surrender to Him.
Perhaps he or she simply needs someone to care enough to look past the false exterior, to keep sharing God's love despite any negative reactions.

So share Christ with others regardless of what you see on the outside, praying that God will meet the true needs of hearts. Who knows? That person you're taking a chance on may turn out to be another Gretchen, someone who will eventually embrace a relationship with God with all her heart.

GRAB YOUR JOURNAL and write to the Lord about witnessing to others. Ask Him to give you the courage to be His ambassador to everyone He places in your path—whether the person seems to be receptive or not.

Chapter 9

Seeing the Truth

1 **WHEN GRETCHEN** came to the Bible study for the first time, everyone was friendly to her, making her feel both welcome and comfortable. Julia was proud of her friends and the way they reached out to Gretchen right away.

All of us have been *the new person* in a group. We can relate to the anxiety of not knowing anyone else or worrying if others will accept us. A kind word or smile when someone first arrives can calm those fears and give that person an immediate sense of belonging.

Tips for making others feel accepted when coming to your youth/college group for the first time:
Welcome and introduce yourself to newcomers.
Reach out to them even if you feel a little awkward at first. Most people do; it's normal!
Invite a visitor to sit with you and your friends.
Help visitors get involved in the activities of the meeting.
Even if you **just smile**, it can make a big difference!

Gretchen certainly responded to the hospitality and friendliness of Julia's friends. Do you think she would have received as much healing from Gary's conversation that night had she not already felt so loved and accepted by the group? Explain your answer.

_____
_____
_____
_____

In the Bible, there is a good example of what a smile can communicate to a person who is feeling nervous about a meeting. It's found in the story of two estranged brothers, Jacob and Esau. Jacob had severely wronged and hurt his brother before fleeing for his life to another land. Now that he was returning home after many years, he was afraid Esau was still angry with him and might even try to kill him. Look below and see how Jacob responded to Esau's greeting when they finally met again:

> **Genesis 33:10b (NLT)**
> "…what a relief to see your friendly smile. It is like seeing the face of God!"

That dreaded moment instantly turned into a beautiful reunion by Esau's simple smile of welcome and acceptance.

For many people, attending a new group is an awkward and dreaded experience. Your smile can be a great relief to them, making them feel almost as if they're seeing the smile of God.

> Again, it doesn't take much to reach out to others and make them feel a part. A smile, a kind word, or an invitation to sit with you goes a long way.

*Never forget how it feels to be the **new girl**.*

> **Luke 6:31 (CEV)**
> Treat others just as you want to be treated.

When you get tempted to skip the effort involved in welcoming new people, take a second and think about how *you* would want to be treated if it were you walking through that door for the first time. Then go ahead and do what you would want done for you in that situation.

GRAB YOUR JOURNAL and write about your willingness to be friendly to others, especially when you don't feel like it. Ask God to give you His love, compassion, and strength to treat others with the dignity and consideration they need.

Seeing the Truth 55

2 ONCE GARY accepted Christ, his group leader warned him that living in the party atmosphere of the frat house would make it extremely difficult for Gary to grow in his relationship with God. Jim knew that most of Gary's frat brothers would not understand his decision to live for Christ. In fact, they would most likely try to draw him back into bad choices.

> **1 Corinthians 15:33b (NLT)**
> Don't be fooled by those who say such things, for "bad company corrupts good character."

*Notice that bad company (spending time with the wrong people) **will** have a negative impact on your good character.*

In order for things to change in Gary's life, *Gary's way of life* needed to change. Once he realized that, he stopped hanging out with people who would work against him. Instead, he surrounded himself with new friends that would *build* his relationship with Christ rather than tear it down. He started changing the things he was doing, how he was spending his time. In the end, he grew to be a great man, one that people could admire for more than just being a good football player.

Ask yourself…
Are there things in my life that my desire to serve Christ is requiring me to change?   _____   _____
Am I listening to the Holy Spirit and making those changes so my life can become all that God has planned?   _____   _____

God only asks you to give up things which will hurt you or hold you back somehow. Whatever He asks you to change will actually make your life better now and in the future. God doesn't take things away without giving you something even better in its place. *Open your heart to what's better!*

GRAB YOUR JOURNAL and write about any area of your life where you might be letting *bad company* influence you. Remember, in addition to friends, the company you keep includes music, TV, movies, magazines, the Internet, and however else you spend your time.

3   **GARY SHARED** with Gretchen the guilt and regret he had felt for the way he treated girls while in his fraternity. He explained it took time before he was able to accept God's forgiveness for what he'd done, that it took even longer to forgive himself.

Why do you think Gary had so much trouble forgiving himself?

_____
_____
_____
_____
_____

Eventually, Gary understood he couldn't change what had already happened. But he *could* surrender to the Lord and make better choices from that day forward. He could ask for forgiveness from the girls he had hurt, sharing the love of Jesus with them and introducing them to a God Who could heal what he couldn't. He could also reach out to others, helping them to avoid making such costly mistakes.

The Bible is full of men and women who made major mistakes in their lives and yet were still loved and used by God.

Take time to read about the lives of these people:	
King David 2 Samuel 11 & 12	He had sex with another man's wife and then had the husband killed to cover up his sin.
Rahab Joshua 2:1-21 Joshua 6:17-25	She was a prostitute before helping the Israelites and then converting to their faith.
The Apostle Paul Acts 8:1-3	Before receiving Christ, he threw Christians in jail, condoning their deaths.
The Apostle Peter Mark 8:31-33 & 14: 66-72	He denied Christ and didn't always do or say the right thing.

These are just a few of the many people recorded in Scripture that failed God at some time in their lives. What was their secret to getting past mistakes? *Having a repentant and submitted heart to the Lord.* As each of these people repented and chose to respect and obey God, they were forgiven, honored, and blessed by the Lord. They allowed God to change them and to *influence their choices from that point on.*

When you read this chapter in the book, did you relate to Gary with your own feelings of guilt and regret over things you've done? Have you tried to change, only to find yourself repeating the same mistakes, feeling guilty all over again? Explain your answers.

_____
_____
_____
_____

Be encouraged: If you come to the Lord, sincerely ask forgiveness for mistakes, and submit to His lordship in your life, *God will give you a new beginning!*

> God loves a humble heart that turns to Him for help. Through His Word, He will give you wisdom to make good decisions **from this point on.**

> ### Isaiah 57:15 (NLT)
> The high and lofty one who lives in eternity, the Holy One, says this: "I live in the high and holy place with those whose spirits are contrite and humble. I restore the crushed spirit of the humble and revive the courage of those with repentant hearts."
>
> ### Isaiah 57:15 (CEV)
> Our holy God...says: Though I live high above in the holy place, I am here to help those who are humble and depend only on me.

GRAB YOUR JOURNAL and write about any guilt or regrets you have regarding things you've done. Give it all to the Father with a repentant heart, and let Him restore your spirit and give you new courage to try again. Know that as you depend on Him, God will help you make better choices starting today!

4   **AS GARY** talked with Gretchen, he encouraged her to think about what she *wanted* to do with her life—not what she thought she *had* to do because of her relationship with Brad. Gary was trying to make her see that what *she thought* she deserved was opposite of what God wanted her to experience.

> Gary was trying to get Gretchen to dream a little, to enlarge her vision and get a glimpse of all the wonderful things God had planned for her. Gary didn't want Gretchen to settle for so little **when God wanted to bless her with so much!**

Important Truth

It's what God says about you and your life that really matters, not how you feel (like Gretchen) or what others think or say!

Has anyone spoken negative things to you about your future, possibly pointing to your family, your race, your level of education, where you live, how much money you have, or something you've done wrong? Did being told how little you can expect out of life discourage your dreams for more? If so, it's time to change your thinking. *Refuse to let other people determine your destiny*—call upon the Creator of the universe to reveal His wonderful, divine plan for you!

Have you struggled with preconceived ideas and low expectations?

For example, maybe your family background has you thinking, "My mom wasn't happily married. Can I expect to be?"

In this situation, you might wonder if it's realistic to hope for a husband who will love and commit to you for a lifetime.

Be assured…

Marriage is God's best scenario for love and romance, so it's available for you if you want it. You have every reason to hope for a happy and lasting marriage.

Seeing the Truth

The key to receiving God's blessings is *knowing what He has promised you* and *believing He will be faithful to do it* (as you cooperate with Him). You can have that kind of confidence because when Jesus died on the cross, He purchased more than just salvation for you.

How do you learn what else Jesus purchased, what else God has for your life? One way is by spending time reading the Bible. It's full of wonderful promises God has made to you—for taking care of you, giving you everything you need, bringing you peace, granting you favor with other people, protecting you, leading and guiding you, giving you wisdom…The list goes on and on.

Think for a minute. Are there any areas of life where, like Gretchen, you've resigned yourself to failure (or just very low expectations)? After our discussion, are you willing to seek God and trust Him for all He has planned for you?

_____

_____

_____

_____

> **Ephesians 3:20-21 (AMP)**
> [20]Now to Him Who, by (in consequence of) the [action of His] power that is at work within us, is able to [carry out His purpose and] do superabundantly, far over and above all that we [dare] ask or think [infinitely beyond our highest prayers, desires, thoughts, hopes, or dreams]--[21]To Him be glory in the church and in Christ Jesus throughout all generations forever and ever. Amen (so be it).

*Isn't it great to know that God wants to do **superabundantly** beyond anything we could ask or dream?*

GRAB YOUR JOURNAL and write about what you want your future to look like. Dream a little! Let your Father enlarge your vision for all *He* has planned for you. Ask Him to show you those plans over time. Commit to trust God for what your heart desires. Don't settle for a little when He has prepared so very much!

Chapter 10

A Night of Regrets

1   IT WAS the night of the big dance, and everything was going smoothly as Julia got ready in her room. Her hair and nails had turned out perfectly, her dress and jewelry were absolutely beautiful, and she had a handsome date waiting for her down in the parlor below. Turning to the mirror for one final glance, Julia reflected on her feelings at that moment. Did she feel the pure happiness she had anticipated? Not really. Why?

Julia said it was because she had always envisioned her parents making a fuss over her and taking lots of pictures before her first dance. That was true, but the main reason was she was missing something she had always enjoyed before—her parents' approval.

When talking with Gretchen, Julia said her mom and dad didn't want her dating or going to dances in high school. Yet nothing was said to indicate the same restrictions applied to her once she was at college. Under the *right* circumstances, her parents might have been happy for her to go to a dance. But because Julia rebelliously kept Jay and her sorority life a secret from them, they were shut out of their daughter's life.

What did Julia realize that evening that we all need to learn?
When you distance yourself from proper authority and choose to rebel, life is never as satisfying. It may be fun for a while, but it brings no lasting peace or satisfaction.
Think back…
Can you relate to Julia's situation? Have you ever gone ahead and done something without your parent/guardian knowing? If so, write how that made you feel:
_____
_____
_____
_____

Now read the following story from the Book of Luke:

> ### Luke 15:11-24 (NLT)
> ¹¹To illustrate the point further, Jesus told them this story: "A man had two sons. ¹²The younger son told his father, 'I want my share of your estate now before you die.' So his father agreed to divide his wealth between his sons. ¹³A few days later this younger son packed all his belongings and moved to a distant land, and there he wasted all his money in wild living. ¹⁴About the time his money ran out, a great famine swept over the land, and he began to starve. ¹⁵He persuaded a local farmer to hire him, and the man sent him into his fields to feed the pigs. ¹⁶The young man became so hungry that even the pods he was feeding the pigs looked good to him. But no one gave him anything. ¹⁷When he finally came to his senses, he said to himself, 'At home even the hired servants have food enough to spare, and here I am dying of hunger! ¹⁸I will go home to my father and say, 'Father, I have sinned against both heaven and you, ¹⁹and I am no longer worthy of being called your son. Please take me on as a hired servant.' ²⁰So he returned home to his father. And while he was still a long way off, his father saw him coming. Filled with love and compassion, he ran to his son, embraced him, and kissed him. ²¹His son said to him, 'Father, I have sinned against both heaven and you, and I am no longer worthy of being called your son.' ²²But his father said to the servants, 'Quick! Bring the finest robe in the house and put it on him. Get a ring for his finger and sandals for his feet. ²³And kill the calf we have been fattening. We must celebrate with a feast, ²⁴for this son of mine was dead and has now returned to life. He was lost, but now he is found.' So the party began."

Here the younger son learned the same lesson as Julia. Although his life of rebellion and wild living was fun for a while, it didn't bring him lasting happiness or satisfaction. In fact, it caused him to eventually lose his entire inheritance, leaving him with absolutely nothing. He became so destitute and hungry, even pig slop looked good to him. Yuck!

> **Rebellion is basically defying or not submitting to proper authority.**

Another way to look at rebellion is simply *acting without the fear of God*. This phrase is often misunderstood. Some people interpret *the fear of God* as being intensely afraid of Him, worrying that with any false move, you'll be instantly struck with lightning! However, that's not what that phrase really means.

Fearing God means recognizing the greatness, power, and holiness of an awesome God and therefore giving Him the reverence and respect He deserves. When we fear God in the right way, we voluntarily accept His authority over us and try to live our lives in a way that will honor Him. That often means bypassing something ungodly that the natural side of us wants to do. Why? Because God is Lord of our lives, we want to please Him, and He's worthy of our best possible behavior.

> **Proverbs 19:23 (NLT)**
> Fear of the Lord leads to life, bringing security and protection from harm.

Fearing God not only keeps us on the right path in life, but it also gives us security and protects us from harm. What great benefits!

Take a moment now to examine your heart. Are there any areas where you don't feel satisfied? If so, ask yourself if you are *fearing the Lord* (honoring and obeying Him) in those areas. Write down your thoughts below:

_____
_____
_____
_____
_____
_____
_____

GRAB YOUR JOURNAL and write down your thoughts about the story of the prodigal son, anything you may have learned from reading it. Thank God for loving you so much, for *always welcoming you back with open arms* when you repent from doing things your own way and return to His presence. Ask the Lord to give you a greater understanding of how to honor and respect Him as you make decisions in life. Know that as you do, you'll stay close to home with your Heavenly Father, where you can enjoy a blessed life filled with satisfaction and protection.

| 2 | **AFTER THE** dance, Jay took Julia down by the lake to propose to her. Before popping the question, he shared some things about his life and childhood he had not previously mentioned. Julia had dated Jay for months without knowing anything about his parents, their unhappy family life, or the rejection and hurt Jay had suffered.

All that Julia knew about Jay was he was fun and good-looking. *She hadn't thought to ask about her boyfriend's background.* If she had, she might have learned earlier about Jay's internal struggles. She knew nothing until that night at the gazebo when he gave her a brief description of his life before coming to college.

What did you think when Jay proposed to Julia and gave her such a beautiful engagement ring? Were you surprised or disappointed when she refused to marry him? Did you feel sorry for Jay?

Sadly, Julia found out too late that simply knowing Jay was handsome and fun *wasn't* enough. His insecurities caused him to use lies and manipulation to get her to do things he wanted. In the end, because he couldn't accept Julia's refusal to his proposal, he tricked her into going to the Eddington Hotel in order to rape her and guilt her into marrying him. *Had Julia better understood the depth of Jay's issues,* she might have been more cautious and made some better choices.

> **Proverbs 26:24-26 (NLT)**
> ²⁴People may cover their hatred with pleasant words, but they're deceiving you. ²⁵They pretend to be kind, but don't believe them. Their hearts are full of many evils. ²⁶While their hatred may be concealed by trickery, their wrongdoing will be exposed in public.

Warning: Get to know a guy before getting involved!

As we saw in the story, Jay was dealing with rejection, resentment, and possibly even hatred toward his parents, yet his speech and conduct didn't reveal it at first. However, as the above Scripture predicted, the true condition of his heart *did* come out in time.

What can you learn from Julia's experience with Jay?

It's really important to **be honest with your parents/guardians** about your dating relationships.

Julia's parents didn't even know about Jay. If she had been honest and given them the chance to get to know him, they might have sensed his instability and foreseen the danger that was to come. The Lord could have used Julia's parents to help her remove the romantic blinders and see the *real* Jay before his first attack on her.

In reading this section, can you see the important role parents/guardians/mentors play in helping you evaluate your relationships? Explain your answer.

_____
_____
_____
_____
_____
_____

A Night of Regrets

> **Warning:** Be careful about getting into a relationship where you only know what the other person shares about himself.

A perfect example is dating via the Internet. When you're getting to know someone online, you only know what that person is telling you. He could be telling you the truth, but it's possible he is lying about his age, appearance, or things he likes to do. He could just be saying what you want to hear, becoming whoever he thinks you want him to be.

> **Don't take foolish chances!**
>
> Many girls have started relationships with guys on the Internet without parent/guardian knowledge. A girl may begin to trust an online boyfriend and even agree to meet him secretly, only to be raped, abducted, or killed. As unthinkable as it is, there are predators on the Internet, men who pretend to be teenagers or "friendly guys" online while searching for girls they can either blackmail or trick into meeting with them in real life (in order to harm them).

> **Psalm 17:7-9 (NLT)**
> [7] Show me your unfailing love in wonderful ways. By your mighty power you rescue those who seek refuge from their enemies. [8] Guard me as you would guard your own eyes. Hide me in the shadow of your wings. [9] Protect me from wicked people who attack me, from murderous enemies who surround me.

When it comes to relationships, we need to be wise. We need to keep reading God's Word and stay close to the Father in prayer so that we can clearly hear the voice of the Holy Spirit and assess situations and people correctly.

GRAB YOUR JOURNAL and write your thoughts on this important subject. Ask God to use His mighty power to protect you from those who would do you harm. Determine to stay within the bounds of godly wisdom and godly authority, knowing God will keep you safe from enemies as you cooperate with Him.

Chapter 11

Making Choices

1 **GRETCHEN TRIED** breaking up with Brad at the restaurant, but when he reacted with angry threats, she realized she needed help. Excusing herself to go to the restroom, she called Gary on her cell phone. Thankfully, he was able to make it to the restaurant in time to help her.

Have you ever found yourself in a real problem situation? Did you ask someone to help you, or did you try to work it out by yourself? What happened?

_____

_____

_____

_____

God says that He is always ready to help you when you are in trouble. He often uses the people in your life to share your problems, big and small.

Psalm 46:1 (NLT)
God is our refuge and strength, always ready to help in times of trouble.

Galatians 6:2 (NLT)
Share each other's burdens, and in this way obey the law of Christ.

Be wise like Gretchen, and don't try to handle difficult issues alone (especially if someone is hurting you or if you are hurting yourself). Whether your situation is critical or not so serious, *everything* that affects you is important to God! There are people all around you that want to see you experience the best life possible. You can talk to a parent, teacher, neighbor, leader at church, or another trusted adult about what you're experiencing. *God can use them to help you get to a safe place,* emotionally and physically.

Making Choices

> Remember what we said in an earlier entry? If you hide problems or hurts, that secrecy gives them the ideal place to tunnel and grow. However, if you tell someone about them, the light of the truth will expose what's happening. Once everything is out in the open, you can get the help you need to be healed and free.

Do you ever feel embarrassed or afraid to admit to your family or leaders that your life isn't perfect? Explain.

_____

_____

_____

_____

It helps to remember...

No one's life is perfect. We all need help from others sometimes. The sooner you seek out help, the sooner you can begin to experience the life God wants you to live.

Jeremiah 29:11 (NLT)
"For I know the plans I have for you," says the Lord. "They are plans for good and not for disaster, to give you a future and a hope."

*God's **good plans** for us will not happen automatically. We must cooperate with Him to see them all come to pass.*

If you are going through something, you need to let someone know. *Start with God.* He already knows your situation, but He wants you to come to Him with it.

GRAB YOUR JOURNAL and write about any areas—big or small—where you need help. Don't wait to deal with things; God wants them to start changing for you *today!* If you need to, ask God to give you the courage to reach out to others for the support you need. Like Gretchen, tell a trusted adult what is going on and let the right people help share your burdens.

2 **IN THIS** chapter, Julia, Fran, and Gretchen talk about premarital sex. Let's start our discussion by defining the word *pure*.

> **According to Merriam-Webster.com,** *pure* **means:** *free from moral fault or guilt.*

Another way to say it might be: *to be innocent of doing wrong.* So let's find out what God says about the sexual relationship (and what *He* considers right and wrong).

Did you know sex causes a man and a woman to become one?

> **Mark 10:6-9 (NLT)**
> ⁶"But 'God made them male and female' from the beginning of creation. ⁷This explains why a man leaves his father and mother and is joined to his wife, ⁸and the two are united into one.' Since they are no longer two but one, ⁹let no one split apart what God has joined together."

Does it surprise you to know that sex was *God's* idea? *And* that He meant it to be an enjoyable part of a married couple's life? In fact, there are some very romantic passages in the Bible (such as in the Song of Solomon and in the Psalms).

> **Hebrews 13:4a (NKJV)**
> Marriage is honorable among all, and the bed undefiled...
>
> **Hebrews 13:4 (NLT)**
> Give honor to marriage, and remain faithful to one another in marriage. God will surely judge people who are immoral and those who commit adultery.

> The above verse (in two translations) says God designed sex for married couples only. In 1 Corinthians 7:5, God actually reminds husbands and wives to have sex *regularly!* But what is the key word in all of this? **Marriage.**

Making Choices

Think about it. Sex is the most intimate thing you can experience with someone; it connects you to him physically, emotionally, and spiritually. In fact, the Bible says sex makes you *one* with a man. It's so powerful, God designed it to be experienced within marriage only, so it can be protected and valued for a lifetime. God wants your wedding bed to be beautiful and pure, an enjoyable but safe and sacred place.

On the flip side, sex outside of marriage is immoral (wrong). Period. God wants us to enjoy sex, but He asks that we enjoy it in marriage, the way He designed it to work best.

What about all the stages between holding hands and actual sexual intercourse? What can be said about those?

How much physical affection do you think is okay before marriage?

_____
_____
_____
_____
_____

When do you think physical contact starts crossing over into premarital sex?

_____
_____
_____
_____
_____
_____

While the Bible may not have a list of dating do's and don'ts, it does give some basic principles to guide you.

> ### 1 Corinthians 6:18-20 (NLT)
> [18]Run from sexual sin! No other sin so clearly affects the body as this one does. For sexual immorality is a sin against your own body. [19]Don't you realize that your body is the temple of the Holy Spirit, who lives in you and was given to you by God? You do not belong to yourself, [20]for God bought you with a high price. So you must honor God with your body.

Now read these additional verses:

1 Thessalonians 4:3-5 (CEV)
[3]God wants you to be holy, so don't be immoral in matters of sex. [4]Respect and honor your body.* [5]Don't be a slave of your desires or live like people who don't know God.   (*see copyright page)

2 Timothy 1:3a (NKJV)
I thank God, whom I serve with a pure conscience…

What is your attitude toward sex? Is it...
How much can I get away with physically before getting into trouble? (Trouble meaning becoming pregnant, contracting a sexually transmitted disease, earning a bad reputation, etc.)
Or is it...
What should I do, Lord, to please You? I am so grateful for who You are in my life. What will make You happy and proud of me as Your daughter? What choices can I make so that I can remain a virgin—or a spiritually restored virgin*—until my wedding night? (*see last journal entry in this chapter)

Making Choices

Determining your attitude *now* is crucial to making the right decisions with your body. As you make choices, remember that the Holy Spirit lives within you now, God paid a tremendous price for you to be His, and He wants you to act in ways that bring honor to Him as well as protect and bless you. We want to serve God with a pure conscience, to be set apart for His purpose and service, to do things the way He instructs us. *There is great benefit and safety in obedience!*

What are some of the serious risks involved with premarital sex?

_____
_____
_____
_____

Keeping that in mind, here are some good guidelines to follow before marriage:

♥ Sexual body parts should be reserved for sex in marriage.
♥ Guard against too much time spent together alone.
♥ If you're not sure the Lord would approve, avoid it.
♥ If you can't do it in faith and good conscience, don't.
♥ If you wouldn't want someone to see you doing it, you probably shouldn't.
♥ Instead of pushing to the very edge of what is permissible, pull back, giving yourself a margin of safety. That way, you'll be able to make it to your wedding night having pleased your Heavenly Father.

GRAB YOUR JOURNAL and write about the Bible verses you read in this entry. What do they mean to you? Next, write to God about the guidelines given. How do you feel about them? Can you think of any others that might help you wait for sex until marriage? Be honest as you journal about this important subject. Ask God to give you the determination, strength, strategies, and wisdom to make the right choices with your body.

3 J ULIA WAS surprised when Fran blurted out she was pregnant in front of Gretchen. During their conversation afterwards, Julia said, "…I guess God tells us to be abstinent for a reason." (The term *abstinent* refers to not having sex.)

Actually, it's important we understand that *everything* God tells us in His Word is *for a reason*. Sometimes we understand His reasoning up front; sometimes we don't. Yet it helps to know God didn't make up a bunch of rules to ruin our fun in life. God's methods have a *purpose*, and that purpose is always for the ultimate good of you and others. Is this a new concept to you? Explain.

Isaiah 55:9 (NLT)
For just as the heavens are higher than the earth, so my ways are higher than your ways and my thoughts higher than your thoughts.

You can confidently trust in God's wisdom. He really does know what He's doing!

In the last entry, we talked about why God reserves sex for marriage. Now let's talk about some specific *benefits* that come from saving sex for your honeymoon:

- ♥ You will enjoy the peace of a clear conscience as you choose to please your Heavenly Father.
- ♥ You avoid the heartbreak that comes from cycling in and out of sexual relationships, one guy after another.
- ♥ You won't become insensitive to the beauty and sacredness of sex.
- ♥ You have no emotional scars or bad memories from previous experiences.
- ♥ You avoid the insecurities that accompany a premarital sexual relationship:
  - ◦ Does he really love me, or does he just want sex?
  - ◦ Do I measure up to the other girls he's slept with?
  - ◦ Will he love me for a lifetime, or find someone else when he gets bored with me?

- ♥ You won't be tempted to lie to your parents/guardians about what you're doing physically.
- ♥ You are protected from sexually transmitted diseases that damage your body and can prevent you from having children later.
- ♥ You are protected from getting pregnant and having to raise a child by yourself.
- ♥ You will be spared problems in your *married* sex life that come from having premarital sexual experiences.
- ♥ You will receive honor by waiting—people will respect you.
- ♥ You have anticipation during your engagement.
- ♥ Your fiancé feels valued because you're waiting to give yourself just to him.
- ♥ You feel valued by your fiancé's choice to wait for you.
- ♥ You will actually be *more* fulfilled sexually after marriage because:
  - ▹ You have God's blessing.
  - ▹ There's no guilt or shame, only enjoyment.
  - ▹ Sex is special because you have something new and exciting to experience together.
  - ▹ You can feel secure knowing you have a lifetime to grow together in your sexual relationship.
- ♥ You have a great story and example for your children.

God does ask you to postpone the pleasure of sex until you're married, but as you can see from this list, it's well worth the wait!

If you mean it from your heart, on the next page, write out your commitment to God to wait for sex until you are married. (Not just a casual, feel-good promise for this moment, but a *purposeful decision* to do whatever it takes to keep your wedding night sacred.) Ask God for *His power* to keep your commitment to Him—*no matter what*. Then find someone you trust who will keep you accountable and will help you when you're tempted to forget the benefits and beauty of saving sex for marriage.

My Pledge to Wait

_____
_____
_____
_____
_____
_____
_____
_____
_____
_____
_____

Date_____ Signed_____

If you're reading all this and are upset because you've already had sexual experiences, be encouraged! *God still has something special for you.* Skip ahead and read the next journal entry right now.

(If this doesn't apply to you, continue journaling below.)

GRAB YOUR JOURNAL and write to the Lord about trusting and following what His Word says, *even if you don't fully understand His reasons* at the time. Then write to Him about the benefits we've discussed for waiting to have sex until marriage. Which ones mean the most to you? Can you think of any others? If you wrote out the pledge above, ask God to help you keep that important commitment. With God and support from others, *you can make it!*

Making Choices

4   SOME OF you may be asking, "What if I've made mistakes and am not a virgin? Is there any hope for me to experience God's best in marriage?" The answer is *absolutely!* Remember Gretchen? She made sexual mistakes with Brad after he raped her, but when she repented and made Jesus her Lord, He forgave her and made a new beginning possible.

> **Psalm 86:5 (NLT)**
> O Lord, you are so good, so ready to forgive, so full of unfailing love for all who ask for your help.

God is ready to forgive any mistakes you have made.

Since Gretchen is a fictional character, let's look at two real women in the Bible who had sexual experiences outside of marriage. Let's see what Jesus' attitude was toward them.

> **John 8:1-11 (NLT)**
> ¹Jesus returned to the Mount of Olives, ²but early the next morning he was back again at the Temple. A crowd soon gathered, and he sat down and taught them. ³As he was speaking, the teachers of religious law and the Pharisees brought a woman who had been caught in the act of adultery. They put her in front of the crowd. ⁴"Teacher," they said to Jesus, "this woman was caught in the act of adultery. ⁵The law of Moses says to stone her. What do you say?" ⁶They were trying to trap him into saying something they could use against him, but Jesus stooped down and wrote in the dust with his finger. ⁷They kept demanding an answer, so he stood up again and said, "All right, but let the one who has never sinned throw the first stone!" ⁸Then he stooped down again and wrote in the dust. ⁹When the accusers heard this, they slipped away one by one, beginning with the oldest, until only Jesus was left in the middle of the crowd with the woman. ¹⁰Then Jesus stood up again and said to the woman, "Where are your accusers? Didn't even one of them condemn you?" ¹¹"No, Lord," she said. And Jesus said, "Neither do I. Go and sin no more."

The men who brought this woman to Jesus were expecting Him to condemn her to death by stoning, as was their law for such a sin. Yet Jesus reacted in an unexpected way. He instructed the stoning to begin by the person in the group of accusers who had never sinned himself. Of course, no one standing there (except Jesus) could boast of never sinning. So no one was able to throw the first stone, and the group of accusing men slowly walked away, one by one.

What did Jesus do next? As the perfect and sinless One, He alone could rightly condemn this woman for her sin. Did he? *No!* When she called Him *Lord*, He said that He *did not* condemn her. Instead, He extended mercy and forgiveness to her and then told her to go and not sin anymore. He wanted her to respond to His love, mercy, and forgiveness *with a lifestyle change.*

> **Romans 8:1 (NLT)**
> So now there is no condemnation for those who belong to Christ Jesus.

Don't let people condemn you. Let Jesus redirect you.

If you have made bad choices sexually like the woman in this story, the best thing you can do is to call out to Jesus as *Lord* and receive His mercy and forgiveness. He won't condemn you; *He loves you!* But since you belong to Jesus, you need to change what you have been doing, live as He directs you, and sin no more in that area.

Take a minute to write down your thoughts about what we've discussed so far.

_____

_____

_____

_____

> **Luke 7:36-40a (NLT)**
> ³⁶One of the Pharisees asked Jesus to have dinner with him, so Jesus went to his home and sat down to eat. ³⁷When a certain immoral woman from that city heard he was eating there, she brought a beautiful alabaster jar filled with expensive perfume. ³⁸Then she knelt behind him at his feet, weeping. Her tears fell on his feet, and she wiped them off with her hair. Then she kept kissing his feet and putting perfume on them. ³⁹When the Pharisee who had invited him saw this, he said to himself, "If this man were a prophet, he would know what kind of woman is touching him. She's a sinner!" ⁴⁰Then Jesus answered his thoughts. "Simon," he said to the Pharisee, "I have something to say to you."
>
> *(continue reading verses 44-50 on next page)*

> **Luke 7:44-50 (NLT)**
> ⁴⁴Then he turned to the woman and said to Simon, "Look at this woman kneeling here. When I entered your home, you didn't offer me water to wash the dust from my feet, but she has washed them with her tears and wiped them with her hair. ⁴⁵You didn't greet me with a kiss, but from the time I first came in, she has not stopped kissing my feet. ⁴⁶You neglected the courtesy of olive oil to anoint my head, but she has anointed my feet with rare perfume. ⁴⁷I tell you, her sins—and they are many—have been forgiven, so she has shown me much love. But a person who is forgiven little shows only little love." ⁴⁸Then Jesus said to the woman, "Your sins are forgiven." ⁴⁹The men at the table said among themselves, "Who is this man, that he goes around forgiving sins?" ⁵⁰And Jesus said to the woman, "Your faith has saved you; go in peace."

Because the word *immoral* is used to describe this second woman, she may have been a prostitute—someone who exchanged sex for pay. How did Jesus respond to her? Did He shun her or reject her because of her sexual sins? Not at all. In fact, He accepted her and allowed her to be close to Him, to touch Him and show her gratitude to Him in her own way. He told her that her sins were forgiven, her faith had saved her, and she should go in peace.

Those are the same things Jesus says to us when we ask God to forgive us of our mistakes and make Him Lord of our lives. He forgives us, saves us by our faith in Him, and then gives us His peace. Like both of these women you read about, He gives us the opportunity to begin afresh in Him. Yet what is God's instruction to us once we have gotten that fresh start?

> **Romans 6:13 (NLT)**
> Do not let any part of your body become an instrument of evil to serve sin. Instead, give yourselves completely to God, for you were dead, but now you have new life. So use your whole body as an instrument to do what is right for the glory of God.

As you do what this verse says and use your body for what's right, you can experience all the great things God has planned for you! Even though you are no longer a physical virgin, you can become a *spiritually-restored virgin*. God's forgiveness gives you the opportunity to have a sacred and beautiful sexual union on your wedding night *now that you are doing things His way.*

Of course, some of the consequences of wrong choices may still remain. For instance, if you've had a child through a premature relationship, that precious life will continue to be an ongoing responsibility. However, God can make life for you and your child what your heart desires if you'll put Him first. *He can make things better than you ever thought possible* if you love Him and live your life for Him.

The good news

No matter what mistakes you've made, you can still experience God's best in marriage. **It's not too late!** As you keep trusting Him, God can bring you a husband that will not be threatened by your past, but who will respect you for making the right choices once you came to God for help. He won't judge you for the decisions you made in an earlier season of your life. Instead, he'll admire and cherish you for *the person you are now.*

Years from now, it will count that you started making good sexual choices today. How will it make a difference to your heart, your husband's heart, and God's heart?

_____

_____

_____

GRAB YOUR JOURNAL and write about the two women's stories included in this entry. Write down the verses that meant the most to you. Ask God to forgive you for past mistakes, and be determined to use your body for what is right. Let Him heal you of past hurts and disappointments. Then choose to follow God into the beautiful future He's prepared for you!

Note: If you did not write out your commitment to God to wait for sex from this day forward and you sincerely want to, go back to that page in the previous section and do it now. Make this a *purposeful decision* to do whatever it takes to keep your wedding night sacred now that you have this fresh start. Ask God for *His power* to keep your commitment to Him—to help you do things His way, *regardless of how you feel* at various moments! You will need to find someone you trust to support you and help keep you on track (especially when you are tempted to overlook your promise to save sex for marriage). *It really is worth the effort it takes to wait!*

Chapter 12

Walking Away

1   **As they** sat together in the library, Julia tried to explain once again to Jay why she didn't want to marry him. In fact, she shared all the wrong things she saw in their relationship, giving several reasons why they needed to break up once and for all.

When Julia explained all that to Jay, did you agree with her? Or did you think she was turning down a great opportunity to marry a handsome, wealthy guy like Jay? Explain your answer.

_____
_____
_____
_____
_____
_____
_____
_____

No matter what Julia said to Jay, he couldn't take her words seriously. In his mind, the fun they had together and the kisses they shared spoke much louder than Julia's words. Besides, if she really did believe all that stuff she was saying, *why had she even dated him?* It made no sense to Jay. He was convinced all her crazy talk was because she was afraid to experience the love that was in her heart for him.

What can we learn from this?

You can say what you believe, but if you aren't living it, it doesn't mean much. What you **say** you believe is proven true or false by what you actually **do**.

> **James 2:14-17 (NLT)**
> ¹⁴What good is it, dear brothers and sisters, if you say you have faith but don't show it by your actions? Can that kind of faith save anyone? ¹⁵Suppose you see a brother or sister who has no food or clothing, ¹⁶and you say, "Good-bye and have a good day; stay warm and eat well"—but then you don't give that person any food or clothing. What good does that do? ¹⁷So you see, faith by itself isn't enough. Unless it produces good deeds, it is dead and useless.

> **2 Corinthians 3:18 (NLT)**
> ¹⁸ So all of us who have had that veil removed can see and reflect the glory of the Lord. And the Lord—who is the Spirit—makes us more and more like him as we are changed into his glorious image.

People usually believe actions over words.

It's critical to understand we don't earn our salvation by the good things we do. Salvation is a free gift based on what *Jesus* did through His death and resurrection. We simply receive it gratefully. So *why are our actions still important?* They reveal that our faith in God is *real*, that it affects our lives both inside and out. (That doesn't mean we never make mistakes in life. It just means our life is becoming *more and more like Christ* as we learn and grow in Him.)

> **Take some time to think about your life.**
> **Are your actions lining up with what you say you believe?**
> Honestly answer this question below.

_____

_____

_____

_____

GRAB YOUR JOURNAL and write about the Scriptures in this entry. If you know your actions aren't lining up with His ways, ask your Heavenly Father to help you in this area. With His strength, you can live out your faith day by day!

2 **AFTER LEAVING** the library, Julia spent some time at the sorority house reflecting on her relationship with Jay. She saw that once she began to get emotionally involved with him, the choices she made were based more on feelings than wisdom. She wasn't making *good decisions*; she was making decisions that *felt good* at the time.

Write about a time when you made a foolish choice because your feelings were influencing you more than good judgment.

_____
_____
_____
_____
_____
_____
_____
_____
_____
_____
_____
_____
_____
_____
_____

We all fight that temptation at one point or another—wanting to do what feels good (even if it isn't the wisest thing to do).

Proverbs 16:25 (NLT)
There is a path before each person that seems right, but it ends in death.

We can't always rely on our own assessment of things.

What seems good at the time may not take us where we want to go. In fact, something that feels right at the moment can actually lead to *death* (negative or destructive circumstances). Now that's serious!

This is why we must be careful to make our decisions based on the Word of God. We can't always trust our feelings; they often change from day to day, situation by situation. However, we can rely on the Word of God to remain steady and sure, to consistently take us in the right direction.

> **Psalm 119:24, 33-35 (NLT)**
> [24]Your laws please me; they give me wise advice.
>
> [33]Teach me your decrees, O Lord; I will keep them to the end. [34]Give me understanding and I will obey your instructions; I will put them into practice with all my heart. [35]Make me walk along the path of your commands, for that is where my happiness is found.

How can I know what God's Word tells me to do?
1. Read the Bible often. Here are a few ideas: • Read a Proverb a day. • Read from the New Testament. (The Book of *John* is a great place to start!) • Read through the Psalms.
2. Buy a daily devotion guide. Look up and read the Scripture references.
3. Read one book of the Bible at a time, using a study guide for each one to help you.

GRAB YOUR JOURNAL and write about the verses in this entry. Are there any situations in your life where you're making decisions more on feelings than on what God's Word tells you to do? Ask God to give you understanding in those areas so you can put His principles into action with all your heart. Even if it seems difficult or feels uncomfortable sometimes, *choose to stay on God's course for you.* Remember, God's path is where your happiness—genuine happiness—is found.

3   **WHEN JULIA** explained about Jay's proposal and the final breakup in the library, Karen responded graciously. She could have said *I told you so* and smugly reminded Julia of her repeated warnings not to get involved with Jay again. Yet she didn't. She simply sealed her lips and let Julia share her heart.

> **Proverbs 11:16a (NLT)**
> A gracious woman gains respect...

A gracious woman is kind and courteous, extending mercy to others, showing them compassion when they've made mistakes.

Karen was gracious during her conversation with Julia, and it caused Julia to admire and appreciate her friend.

Good questions to ask yourself

Do I consistently show kindness and courtesy to others?
Do I have compassion for those who've made mistakes?
Can I resist saying *I told you so* when things go like I said they would?

Your response:
_____
_____
_____
_____

Making and keeping friends takes effort and lots of the God kind of love. But good friends are worth it!

Proverbs 17:9 (CEV)
You will keep your friends if you forgive them, but you will lose your friends if you keep talking about what they did wrong.

Ephesians 4:2 (NLT)
Always be humble and gentle. Be patient with each other, making allowance for each other's faults because of your love.

Have you ever had a friend who, when things got heated between you, brought up past arguments or issues? If so, how did that make you feel? How does forgiveness play a part in *making allowance for each other's faults?*

_____
_____
_____
_____
_____
_____
_____
_____
_____

Do you need to be more patient or gentle with your friends? Do you wish any of your friends was more patient or gentle with you? Explain.

_____
_____
_____
_____
_____
_____
_____
_____
_____

GRAB YOUR JOURNAL and write about the verses in this entry, recording your thoughts on each one. Then thank God for always being gracious and merciful toward you. Ask Him to *help you to be a gracious woman*, overlooking faults and loving other people despite their imperfections. Hopefully, true friends are doing the same for you!

Chapter 13

One Last Date

1 **WHEN JAY** asked Julia to go on one last date with him, she hesitated. She didn't want to go, but she saw Jay wanted his first night with his parents to be unspoiled by the news of their breakup. Knowing she had hurt Jay in the past from selfishness, Julia felt obligated to put her own wants aside and help him out one last time. Reluctantly, she agreed to go to dinner with Jay and his parents. While Julia's intentions were good, she didn't understand an important principle: *pleasing God is more important than pleasing other people.*

> **Galatians 1:10 (CEV)**
> I am not trying to please people. I want to please God. Do you think I am trying to please people? If I were doing that, I would not be a servant of Christ.

Julia knew she should end her relationship with Jay once and for all. Going out with him again, no matter what the reason, would mean compromising what she knew was right. Furthermore, helping Jay to deceive his parents about the status of their relationship would be disobeying what the Bible says about honoring parents. No matter how disappointing or uncomfortable it would be for Jay to tell his parents the truth, *they deserved to be treated honestly.* So by helping Jay deceive them, even if only for one night, Julia would be joining in his disobedience. To please Jay, she would have to displease God.

> **1 Thessalonians 2:4b (NLT)**
> Our purpose is to please God, not people. He alone examines the motives of our hearts.

We find out later that the whole situation was a lie anyway; Jay's parents weren't even in the country! Did you sense trouble ahead for Julia on this last date, or were you as shocked as she was when she arrived at the hotel room?

_____
_____
_____
_____
_____

Simple Truth
Sometimes we're tempted to compromise what's right in order to protect what people think of us. So to avoid being misunderstood, we disobey what we know God wants us to do.
Examples
If I don't let her cheat off my paper, she'll think I'm a goody-goody that looks down on her.
I know I'm the manager, but if I report Jake's being late all the time like I'm supposed to, he'll think I'm a mean person on a power trip!
Wrong Choice
playing it safe to please people
Right Choice
pleasing the One who really knows our motives

Had Julia said *no* to Jay, he would've been disappointed and maybe even thought bad of her, that she was selfish to refuse to help him. Yet Julia could have held her head high knowing God knew the truth: She wasn't being selfish; she was being obedient. And in the end, she would not have experienced that hotel nightmare. Remember, God knew *Jay's* true motives, too.

So when you choose to obey God, you may be misunderstood or judged wrongly. But more than likely, over time people will see the real you and the purity of your motives. As in Julia's case, obeying your Heavenly Father might save you from a life-threatening situation you're not even aware of at the time.

GRAB YOUR JOURNAL and write about being someone who tries to please God *more than anyone else.* Ask God to forgive you for the times you've given in to the pressure to please others at His expense. Ask Him to show you how to be sensitive and kind to others as you obey, letting Him take care of the rest.

2 **WHEN YOU** were reading the book, did you notice that each time Julia was about to make a wrong choice or get involved in the wrong thing, *the Lord sent her a warning?* Sometimes it came from the Holy Spirit within her (like before her last date with Jay in this chapter), and other times it came through conversations with people like her parents, Karen, or Gretchen. Regardless, God always reached out to Julia to help her make the right decision and avoid making the wrong one. Unfortunately, Julia often chose to *ignore God* and simply do what she wanted or thought was best at the time. In every situation where that happened, something bad came of it.

Julia's example shows us how important it is to *respond to the voice of the Lord* in our lives. God is always talking to us, trying to protect us, lead us, guide us, and teach us. *It's our choice whether or not we listen and obey.* Since God only wants good things for us, why do you think anyone would choose *not* to listen to and obey God?

_____
_____
_____
_____
_____
_____
_____

Proverbs 8:32-36 (NLT)
³²"And so, my children, listen to me, for all who follow my ways are joyful. ³³Listen to my instruction and be wise. Don't ignore it. ³⁴Joyful are those who listen to me, watching for me daily at my gates, waiting for me outside my home! ³⁵For whoever finds me finds life and receives favor from the Lord. ³⁶But those who miss me injure themselves..."

In these verses, Wisdom invites us to listen to and follow God's instruction, receiving joy, life, and favor when we do. We are warned that those who ignore the wisdom of God only hurt themselves.

> Discipline is all about training someone to be the best that they can be. It sometimes involves necessary correction. Those who discipline us are showing they care about us enough to teach us skills we need to succeed in life.

How do *you* receive discipline from those in authority over you? Do you feel valuable and loved or just restricted and picked on?

_____

_____

_____

Like us, earthly authorities are imperfect and often fail to discipline us correctly or with the right attitude. That's life. Not so with God. He is the perfect disciplinarian, dealing with us in the right way, every time. He knows best in every situation and isn't affected by our out-of-control emotions or bad attitudes. *He keeps working with us* until we finally pass each test! It's up to us *how long* it takes for us to pass every test. But our Heavenly Father is patient with us because *He loves us* and we are worth His time and attention.

> **Proverbs 3:11-12 (NLT)**
> ¹¹My child, don't reject the Lord's discipline, and don't be upset when he corrects you. ¹²For the Lord corrects those he loves, just as a father corrects a child in whom he delights.

When you realize that God corrects you because He loves you, it becomes easier to obey. You begin to see His inner promptings and outer warnings as protection for your life.

Learn to quickly respond to the conviction of the Holy Spirit, knowing you'll always be rewarded in the end.

> **Psalm 27:8 (NLT)**.
> My heart has heard you say, "Come and talk with me." And my heart responds, "Lord, I am coming."

GRAB YOUR JOURNAL and write about your responsiveness to God's voice. Do you stop and listen when He speaks to you about a situation? Do you pay close attention to His warnings? Choose to hear His voice as you read the Bible. Learn to answer, *"Lord, I'm coming,"* when you hear your Father call!

3 **WHEN JULIA** told her roommate about going out with Jay one more time, she was a little disappointed Fran simply told her to have fun. She was used to having a friend like Karen who would try to talk her out of things that were unwise. Julia was expecting Fran to act like her Christian friends, to influence her in the same way. For a moment, she forgot that she and Fran were coming from totally different perspectives, that they had different values and goals in life.

> **2 Corinthians 6:14 (NKJV)**
> Do not be unequally yoked together with unbelievers. For what fellowship has righteousness with lawlessness? And what communion has light with darkness?

What does *yoked* mean? In the literal sense, it's talking about when two oxen would be hooked into in a yoke (wooden frame) so they could evenly pull a load behind them as one unit. In the figurative sense, being *yoked* with someone is being so close to that person, you're moving in the same direction as one unit.

The Bible warns us not to be *unequally yoked* with unbelievers. In other words, if we join ourselves in close friendships with them, it will be unequal. Like Julia and Fran, we won't be pulling together in the same way, in the same direction.

> **Don't misunderstand...**
> We need to be loving and kind to all the people in our lives, sharing with them the good news of Christ and acting as Jesus would toward them.
>
> **But it matters who our best friends are.**

The reason we need our closest friends to also be Christians is so we can encourage each other, pray for each other, and help each other grow—just as Karen did for Julia. Even Jesus reserved his intimate friendship for the twelve disciples.

> **Warning:** If you choose to ignore 2 Corinthians 6:14 and make non-Christians your best friends, they will eventually negatively affect your thinking and actions.

Who do you think had the greater influence on the decisions Julia made about Jay—Fran and her other sorority sisters or Karen and her Christian friends? Why?

_____

_____

_____

_____

_____

_____

_____

> **Proverbs 12:26 (NLT)**
> The godly give good advice to their friends; the wicked lead them astray.

The right friends won't lead you astray (where you shouldn't go).

Take a few minutes to think about your current relationships. Write down the names of your closest friends:	
Name	Is he/she serving Christ?
	☐ Yes ☐ No
	☐ Yes ☐ No
	☐ Yes ☐ No
	☐ Yes ☐ No
	☐ Yes ☐ No
	☐ Yes ☐ No
If any of the friends you just listed are not serving Christ, you can love them, pray for them, and share the Gospel with them, but they should not be the people you spend most of your time with—not your very best friends. You need relationships that will keep you going in the right direction with God.	

GRAB YOUR JOURNAL and write about friendships. If you know you need new friends, trust God to help you find some. It might take a little time, but He will bring them to you if you ask!

4   JULIA FELT she should tell her friends about her dinner date with Jay, but she was too embarrassed to say anything. She couldn't bring herself to admit to Karen and Gretchen that she was seeing Jay *one more time*.

> **Ecclesiastes 4:9-12 (NLT)**
> ⁹**Two people are better off than one, for they can help each other succeed.** ¹⁰If one person falls, the other can reach out and help. But someone who falls alone is in real trouble. ¹¹Likewise, two people lying close together can keep each other warm. But how can one be warm alone? ¹²**A person standing alone can be attacked and defeated, but two can stand back-to-back and conquer.** Three are even better, for a triple-braided cord is not easily broken.

Can you see how important it is to *have good friends by your side?* Had Julia confided in Karen and Gretchen about her date, they probably would have reminded her of the danger of going anywhere with Jay. *They could have helped her fight off the temptation to see him again*—no matter what the reason. (Remember, Julia was only going with Jay to be nice.) Because Julia refused to swallow her pride and share her plans with her friends, she found herself in real trouble later.

Has your pride ever kept *you* from telling the truth when you should have? Explain.

_____
_____
_____

> Value the good friends in your life. Determine to be honest with them even when it's embarrassing or uncomfortable. People can't help you if they don't know what you're struggling with or what's really going on. Like we said in the previous entry, if you don't have a Christian friend to stand by you during difficult times, continue to pray and ask God to bring you one.

GRAB YOUR JOURNAL and write about these verses in Ecclesiastes. Choose to be a good support to your friends, extending a hand when they fall and standing back-to-back with them to help conquer whatever they may be facing. Ask God to strengthen you to swallow your pride and ask for help when you need it, too.

Chapter 14

Heavenly Assistance

1 **WHEN GARY** backtracked to the hotel to thank *Daryl* (the man at the front desk who had helped them find Julia), he was told that no one by that name worked there.

Julia's mom believed Daryl was an angel sent by God to help save her daughter that night. Were you surprised to hear that? What do *you* believe about angels?

_____

_____

_____

_____

_____

_____

For many of us, the word *angel* conjures up the image of a sweet, curly-haired baby with wings sitting on a puffy cloud somewhere. Yet the Bible is full of stories of angels, and none of them fit that timid image.

Psalm 103:20-21 (NLT)
[20]Praise the Lord, you angels, you mighty ones who carry out his plans, listening for each of his commands. [21]Yes, praise the Lord, you armies of angels who serve him and do his will!

Hebrews 1:14 (NLT)
Therefore, angels are only servants—spirits sent to care for people who will inherit salvation.

These three verses describe angels as mighty beings that carry out the plans of God. They are sent to care for people who have accepted God's salvation.

> As a Christian, you can be sure that God has angels assigned to care for **you.** Exciting to think about, isn't it?

Have *you* asked Jesus to forgive your sins and be your Savior? Describe how and when you did. If you haven't yet, would you like to?

_____
_____
_____
_____
_____
_____
_____
_____
_____
_____
_____
_____

> If you would like to give your heart to Jesus and know you are forgiven and accepted into the family of God, turn to *Accepting Christ* in the back of this workbook to learn how.

Ephesians 6:12-13 (NLT)
¹²For we are not fighting against flesh-and-blood enemies, but against evil rulers and authorities of the unseen world, against mighty powers in this dark world, and against evil spirits in the heavenly places. ¹³Therefore, put on every piece of God's armor so you will be able to resist the enemy in the time of evil. Then after the battle you will still be standing firm.

Have you ever considered that in life, we're fighting against more than what we can see with our eyes?

Do you find it comforting to know God has given you His armor to stand against any attack that comes your way? Look up *Ephesians 6:10-18* and list the different pieces of armor we've been given. (Example: *helmet of salvation*)

_____
_____
_____
_____
_____
_____
_____
_____
_____

> Not only has our Father provided us with powerful armor, but He has also sent angels to help us in the fight! We are not fighting alone.

Even Jesus was assisted by an angel while preparing for His greatest challenge: dying on the cross for us.

> **Luke 22:39-43 (NLT)**
> [39] Then, accompanied by the disciples, Jesus left the upstairs room and went as usual to the Mount of Olives. [40] There he told them, "Pray that you will not give in to temptation." [41] He walked away, about a stone's throw, and knelt down and prayed, [42] "Father, if you are willing, please take this cup of suffering away from me. Yet I want your will to be done, not mine." [43] Then an angel from heaven appeared and strengthened him.

GRAB YOUR JOURNAL and write about these verses and the armor God's given you to wear. Thank Him for sending His angels to protect and strengthen you in the battles of life.

2   L‍YING IN her hospital bed, Julia tearfully asked her family and friends to forgive her for the wrong way she had handled things. Her dad assured her that everyone did forgive her, that they were all grateful for her safety.

Have you ever made a big mistake and had to ask someone to forgive you? Explain.

_____

_____

_____

_____

It feels so wonderful to be forgiven, *especially when you didn't feel you deserved it!*

Psalm 86: 4-5 (NLT)
⁴Give me happiness, O Lord, for I give myself to you. ⁵O Lord, you are so good, so ready to forgive, so full of unfailing love for all who ask for your help.

Since God is always ready to forgive us, we should be willing to freely forgive others.

Ephesians 4:32 (AMP)
And become useful and helpful and kind to one another, tenderhearted (compassionate, understanding, loving-hearted), forgiving one another [readily and freely], as God in Christ forgave you.

Mark 11:25 (CEV)
Whenever you stand up to pray, you must forgive what others have done to you. Then your Father in heaven will forgive your sins.

GRAB YOUR JOURNAL and write about these verses, what they mean to you. Thank God for being so good, for *always* being ready to forgive your mistakes, no matter what they are. Receive His joy as you are reminded of His love and mercy toward you. Then choose to *quickly forgive others* from your heart when they wrong you. Not only will you be releasing them for their benefit, you'll also be putting yourself in a place of peace (a place that allows your own sins to be forgiven by your Heavenly Father).

Chapter 15

Necessary Consequences

1   **JULIA'S FATHER** had a long talk with her in the hospital. He had made some important decisions about her future and shared with her some important lessons. Recap what he said to Julia and what you thought about the way he dealt with her mistakes.

_____
_____
_____
_____
_____
_____
_____
_____
_____
_____
_____
_____

Trying to process all that happened to her with Jay, Julia asked her father if he thought Jay had really accepted Christ down at the altar that Sunday. Her dad responded that *no one except God knows for sure when that happens* since it takes place inside of a person. He also said that the *fruit of a person's life* will eventually reveal whether there's been a true change on the inside.

> Julia's dad isn't referring here to natural fruit like apples or oranges; he's talking about figurative fruit, *what a person says and does.*

Necessary Consequences

In other words, when a spiritual change has taken place on the inside of a person, it should eventually show on the outside, too. Because of this, Julia's dad *didn't* think Jay had genuinely made Jesus the Lord of His life when he went down to the altar. His actions never reflected an inward change; his life continued to produce *rotten fruit* (ignoring Julia's wishes, lying to her, drugging her, attempting to rape her, etc.).

Here the Lord talks to us about identifying people by the fruit of their lives. People may seem to be a certain way initially, but their words and actions over time will eventually confirm who they really are.

> **Matthew 7:15-20 (NLT)**
> [15]"Beware of false prophets who come disguised as harmless sheep but are really vicious wolves. [16]You can identify them by their fruit, that is, by the way they act. Can you pick grapes from thorn bushes, or figs from thistles? [17]A good tree produces good fruit, and a bad tree produces bad fruit. [18]A good tree can't produce bad fruit, and a bad tree can't produce good fruit. [19]So every tree that does not produce good fruit is chopped down and thrown into the fire. [20]Yes, just as you can identify a tree by its fruit, so you can identify people by their actions."

> **Galatians 5:22-23 (NLT)**
> [22]But the Holy Spirit produces this kind of fruit in our lives: love, joy, peace, patience, kindness, goodness, faithfulness, [23]gentleness, and self-control...

Stop for a moment to reflect on each quality listed.

Sometimes we read through that list a little too quickly, without realizing that the fruit of God's Spirit reveals the inside of God—*who He really is*. Isn't our God awesome to have such wonderful attributes? Isn't it good to know we don't have the pressure of producing God's fruit on our own? This verse says that *the Holy Spirit* produces those wonderful qualities in our lives. *All we have to do is cooperate with Him!* As we do, we'll see ourselves growing in those qualities more and more.

GRAB YOUR JOURNAL and write about the verses above. Jot down the fruits of the Spirit others can definitely see in you right now. Well done! Next, write the fruits you need to cooperate more with God on, so He can bring them out even more.

2 **SPENDING TIME** with her mom in the hotel reminded Julia of the close relationship they had always shared. She realized her mom was more to her than a great parent; she was a good friend as well. In the blur of the last semester, she had foolishly forgotten that.

When we are focused on the wrong things, it's easy to *foolishly forget* what was once precious to us. Has that ever happened to you? Explain.

_____

_____

_____

_____

> Human nature tends to zoom in on the negative, obsessing about what's wrong and forgetting all about the positives that are happening as well.

> **Psalm 103:1-5 (NKJV)**
> ¹Bless the LORD, O my soul; and all that is within me, bless His holy name! ²Bless the LORD, O my soul, and forget not all His benefits: ³Who forgives all your iniquities, Who heals all your diseases, ⁴Who redeems your life from destruction, Who crowns you with lovingkindness and tender mercies, ⁵Who satisfies your mouth with good things, so that your youth is renewed like the eagle's.

The Psalmist David tells himself not to forget the good things that God does for him. Apparently, he recognizes how easy it is *to get caught up in the struggles of life* and forget the many benefits of belonging to God. In fact, he dedicates an entire chapter to remembering, to listing all the wonderful things God has done, is doing, and will continue to do for those who fear Him. If you have given your life to Christ and made Him your Savior and Lord, *that includes you!*

On the next page, take a moment to list some good things in your life right now. Try to find sixteen things. That may seem like a lot at first, but when you start to be thankful for things like having food to eat today or being able to see the words on this page, the list will grow quickly!

GOOD THINGS IN MY LIFE
1.
2.
3.
4.
5.
6.
7.
8.
9.
10.
11.
12.
13.
14.
15.
16.

GRAB YOUR JOURNAL and write about all you are thankful for today. Refuse to *foolishly forget* the benefits of your relationship with God, and like David, remind yourself of them often.

Chapter 16

Girl Talk

1   **IN THEIR** long talk at the restaurant, Julia's mom summed up her daughter's last semester in one sentence: *You made a lot of wrong choices.*

As His creation, one of the most wonderful gifts God has given us is the freedom to choose. Because He truly loves us, God gives us the freedom to decide whether or not we will love Him, seek Him, serve Him, and live our lives the way He designed. *The choice is entirely up to us;* He won't force us. Even though He knows that His ways, as presented in the Bible, will bring us happiness and true satisfaction, He still gives us the freedom to go our own way any time we choose. All the while, however, He continues reaching out to us, inviting us to take advantage of the peace and wisdom we find in His presence and through obeying His Word.

Having the freedom to make our own choices is two-sided.	
If we choose well, we'll enjoy the benefits of those good choices.	If we choose poorly, we have to live out those negative consequences as well.

> **Deuteronomy 30:19-20 (NLT)**
> [19]"Today I have given you the choice between life and death, between blessings and curses. Now I call on heaven and earth to witness the choice you make. Oh, that you would choose life, so that you and your descendants might live! [20]You can make this choice by loving the Lord your God, obeying him, and committing yourself firmly to him. This is the key to your life…"

Each choice we make either leads to life (something positive) or death (something negative). God loves us so much that He urges us to choose life! He also loves us so much, He lets us choose for ourselves.

Are you glad God has given you freedom to choose? Why or why not?

_____

_____

_____
_____
_____
_____

TIME TO CHOOSE	
Read the following list. Check off areas where you need to start making better choices to secure a great future.	
time spent with God	☐
effort at school	☐
quality of friends	☐
dating relationships	☐
relationship with parents/guardians	☐
what I do for fun	☐
what I do with my body	☐
what I put into my mind	☐
being responsible	☐
being truthful	☐
being thankful	☐
good work ethic	☐
life priorities	☐

GRAB YOUR JOURNAL and write about what you checked in the above chart. Ask God to help you improve those areas, and pick the one you want to work on first. *Write down one better choice you can make this week.* Keep making better choices until you feel that area is strong and healthy. Then come back to this list and focus on another area. Eventually, you will tackle them all. Remember, each choice you make in life (positive or negative) takes you somewhere. *Make sure you like where you're headed!*

2 **WHEN JULIA** asked how she could have had feelings of love for Jay without wanting to marry him, her mom explained that what Julia felt for Jay was more infatuation than love.

Write out a dictionary definition of *infatuation*. Is this genuine love? Or is it merely what we see in romantic movies and novels—just a bunch of fluttery feelings that temporarily put our senses in a whirl?

_____

_____

_____

_____

_____

_____

_____

> The Bible is full of references to love and what it really means, but a great place to find God's definition is **1 Corinthians 13** (what many people call the Love Chapter).

> ### 1 Corinthians 13:4-7 (NLT)
> ⁴Love is patient and kind. Love is not jealous or boastful or proud ⁵or rude. It does not demand its own way. It is not irritable, and it keeps no record of being wronged. ⁶It does not rejoice about injustice but rejoices whenever the truth wins out. ⁷Love never gives up, never loses faith, is always hopeful, and endures through every circumstance.

Think about how our world would change for the better if everyone loved God's way!

God's kind of love is based upon *more than physical attraction or emotion.* It's an *enduring* love that puts the other person first, never gives up, and is committed beyond feelings. It is on this solid foundation that married couples can build their lives (while also experiencing the fluttery feelings and passion enjoyed in romance and sexual intimacy).

> The Song of Solomon in the Bible describes marital love beautifully.

Loving like God doesn't come naturally; it's a conscious choice that requires you to die to your own selfish wants in order to serve others. To love this way, you have to continually lean on the Lord for strength. But without a doubt, it's well worth the effort!

Think about the way *you* love for a moment. Are you patient with others? Would people consider you kind? What about irritable? Are you keeping a scorecard of what others have done against you? Write your honest response to these questions.

_____
_____
_____
_____
_____
_____
_____
_____
_____
_____
_____

> **Remember**: Learning to love like God is a lifelong pursuit. Don't expect to do it perfectly every time—the more you practice it, however, the easier it becomes.

GRAB YOUR JOURNAL and re-read the definition of love in *1 Corinthians 13*. Write down one aspect of His love that you already do well. Thank God for it! Now pick an area where you can improve. All of us have some element that needs work. Ask God to help you grow in loving the way He does.

3 **JULIA'S MOM** talked about taking a man's spiritual temperature to find out if he is hot, cold, or lukewarm toward the Lord. She shared that the time to do this is in the *friendship stage* of a boyfriend/girlfriend relationship, *before* you become emotionally involved. She explained that once romantic feelings enter the picture, it's harder to be objective and honestly evaluate each other.

List other things Julia's mom said that made an impact on you:

_____
_____
_____
_____
_____
_____
_____
_____
_____
_____
_____
_____

Julia's mother got her "spiritual temperature" principle from the following verses:

> **Revelation 3:15-16 (NLT)**
> [15]"I know all the things you do, that you are neither hot nor cold. I wish that you were one or the other! [16]But since you are like lukewarm water, neither hot nor cold, I will spit you out of my mouth!"

Here Jesus talks about spiritual temperature. He says He wants people to be hot or cold, not lukewarm.

Think about a time you had a cold drink on a really hot day. Wasn't it refreshing? Have you ever sipped a piping hot cup of coffee, tea, or cocoa? Wasn't it soothing? Compared to those two extremes, lukewarm liquid is rather disgusting. It certainly isn't as satisfying or as enjoyable to the person drinking it. In fact, Jesus says that He will *spit that type of person out of His mouth* (not want to fellowship with him or her as long as he or she remains lukewarm). No Christian should want Jesus to feel that way about his or her spiritual commitment! So, how do we avoid being lukewarm? Maybe the answer lies in the verses that come afterward.

> **Revelation 3:19-20 (NLT)**
> [19]"I correct and discipline everyone I love. So be diligent and turn from your indifference. [20]Look! I stand at the door and knock. If you hear my voice and open the door, I will come in, and we will share a meal together as friends."

Jesus is saying that He wants us to become *diligent* (to act in ways that show we take our relationship with Him seriously) and to stop being complacent toward Him. He says that He's knocking on the doors of our hearts to be with us. We stop being lukewarm when we choose to open the door and spend time with Him, *when we make Him our priority.* As always, God is willing; yet the choice is up to us.

How would you describe *your* spiritual temperature? Before answering, ask God to help you honestly evaluate if you've become lukewarm.

_____

_____

_____

_____

_____

GRAB YOUR JOURNAL and write about your relationship with the Lord. If you feel you've gotten away from seeking Him (reading His Word yourself, talking to Him in prayer, meeting with other believers at church, etc.), then simply ask for forgiveness and choose to change. *Open the door to your heart.* As you get to know Him more and more, your temperature will be right where it needs to be!

4 **JULIA'S MOM** spent a lot of time explaining relationships. She emphasized that our relationship with God is the only one that's guaranteed; we can rely upon the Lord completely.

> **Hebrews 13:5b-6 (AMP)**
> [5]...for He [God] Himself has said, I will not in any way fail you *nor* give you up nor leave you without support. [I will] not, [I will] not, [I will] not in any degree leave you helpless nor forsake nor let [you] down (relax My hold on you)! [Assuredly not!] [6]So we take comfort and are encouraged and confidently and boldly say, The Lord is my Helper; I will not be seized with alarm [I will not fear or dread or be terrified]. What can man do to me?

*Unlike imperfect people, God will **never** let us down.*

Your Heavenly Father will always love you, no matter what you do or what happens to you. How does it feel to know that *God will always be with you*, that He'll never turn from you or leave you all alone?

_____

_____

_____

_____

_____

_____

_____

_____

_____

GRAB YOUR JOURNAL and read through the verses in this entry again, thinking about each statement. Thank the Lord for loving you so much, for promising to never leave you or relax His hold on your life. If you've been fighting alarm, fear, or dread in some area of your life, give it over to Him, knowing *the God of the universe is your helper!*

Chapter 17

Looking Ahead

1 **IN THIS** chapter, Julia stops to think about her mother—what an amazing and unselfish person she was. Julia had been focused on herself for so long, she had failed to truly appreciate her mom. Think for a moment. Is there anyone in *your* life you've forgotten to appreciate lately?

_____
_____
_____
_____
_____
_____
_____

Thinking back to their conversation in Chapter 16, Julia remembered her mom saying that Julia had *lost Jesus as her first love* during her time at college. Her mom was referring to a message that Jesus sent to one of His churches:

> **Revelation 2:2-5 (NLT)**
> ²"I know all the things you do. I have seen your hard work and your patient endurance. I know you don't tolerate evil people. You have examined the claims of those who say they are apostles but are not. You have discovered they are liars. ³You have patiently suffered for me without quitting. ⁴But I have this complaint against you. You don't love me or each other as you did at first! ⁵Look how far you have fallen! Turn back to me and do the works you did at first. If you don't repent, I will come and remove your lampstand from its place among the churches."

> This church was actually doing a lot of things right! Even so, what was most important to Jesus was that they *truly loved Him and each other.*

> **Revelation 2:4 (AMP)**
> But I have this [one charge to make] against you: that you have left (abandoned) the love that you had at first [you have deserted Me, your first love].

We should love Jesus above anyone or anything else.

When we love the Lord with all our heart, we try our best to imitate Him, to do what we know *He* would do. While our actions are important to Him, what does Jesus want the *most* from us? According to Revelation 2:4, *He wants to be our first love!* Many times we only consider how much we need the Lord and His great love for us. Can you see how important *your* love is *to Him?* Apparently, Jesus feels dishonored in His relationship with us when we go through the motions without lovingly connecting with Him.

> Knowing how important *your love* is to Jesus should make you feel incredibly treasured and special!

As Julia truthfully evaluated her relationship with Jesus, she realized that even though she had received Christ as her Savior and had been raised in a Christian home, she had never taken the time to develop Jesus as her first love. She gave some reasons why she thought she hadn't. What were they?

_____

_____

_____

_____

_____

GRAB YOUR JOURNAL and write about your relationship with Jesus. Like Julia, He's probably one of your loves, but which one? First? Second? Last? Choose to put your relationship with Christ *first* in your heart. Not only will you get to know God better, you'll also find that *making good choices becomes much easier.* After all, when Jesus is truly your Lord, your life can't help but show it!

2 **BY THE** end of this chapter, Julia had sincerely asked for forgiveness for her mistakes during the past semester. She was determined to go home and take time to know her Lord, making Jesus her *first* love. Suddenly, she felt something like a cleansing shower sweep through her. She said it was *the peace that accompanies a clear conscience.*

Share a time when admitting a mistake and asking for forgiveness brought you peace and cleansed your conscience.

_____

_____

_____

_____

_____

_____

> Julia went to sleep in this chapter full of hope, believing God would heal her heart and see her through all the adventures that awaited her back home.

Romans 15:13 (NLT)
I pray that God, the source of hope, will fill you completely with joy and peace because you trust in him. Then you will overflow with confident hope through the power of the Holy Spirit.

Ephesians 1:18 (CEV)
My prayer is that light will flood your hearts and that you will understand the hope that was given to you when God chose you. Then you will discover the glorious blessings that will be yours together with all of God's people.

GRAB YOUR JOURNAL and write what these prayers mean to you. Ask God to flood your heart with His light so you can understand the wonderful future He has prepared for you. Choose to believe in Him, trusting Him to keep you happy, full of peace, and *overflowing with hope* through the power of His Holy Spirit.

Novel 2

Chapter 1

Starting Over

✦ AS NOVEL two opens, Julia has returned home to continue school at a university in her hometown. Why was Julia switching colleges? Was she happy about it?

_____
_____
_____
_____
_____

What was your first impression of Flip? Did it change as you read the novel?

_____
_____
_____
_____
_____

> **Philippians 3:13 (NLT)**
> No dear brothers and sisters, I have not achieved it, but I focus on this one thing: Forgetting the past and looking forward to what lies ahead…

> Forgetting past hurts and mistakes isn't always easy. It takes time and determination (and doesn't mean you will no longer remember what happened). But if you trust God, refuse to dwell on the past, and receive His love, strength, and wisdom to continue on, those painful memories will lose their power to harass you and keep you from enjoying a blessed life.

> **James 5:16a (AMP)**
> Confess to one another therefore your faults (your slips, your false steps, your offenses, your sins) and pray [also] for one another, that you may be healed and restored [to a spiritual tone of mind and heart].

When she first came home, Julia was dealing with hurt feelings and a lot of regret about what had happened with Jay at Tyler. This verse gives the Biblical prescription for getting back on track.

Do you confess your faults to others when you make mistakes? Do you see how prayer helps you heal and continue on? Write down the names of two people you trust to pray for you when you know you've blown it:

_____
_____
_____

What excuse was Julia using to hid Jay's note and pictures from her parents? Was that the real reason? If not, what was?

_____
_____
_____
_____
_____

How good it feels to admit mistakes and ask for forgiveness! Few things feel better than clearing a guilty conscience.

> **Psalm 32:5 (NLT)**
> Finally, I confessed all my sins to you and stopped trying to hide my guilt. I said to myself, "I will confess my rebellion to the Lord." And you forgave me! All my guilt is gone.

GRAB YOUR JOURNAL and write about a time when you felt the relief of both confessing a mistake and being forgiven.

Chapter 2

Bittersweet Reunion

✧ **DID YOU** know that the name *Julia* means *youthful?* Interestingly, a lot of Julia's wrong choices came from being young and immature. For instance, when she hid what she was doing at Tyler from her parents, she almost lost her life. Now she was home again and *still* hiding things from them!

Psalm 139:1-12 (NLT)
[1]O LORD, you have examined my heart and know everything about me. [2]You know when I sit down or stand up. You know my thoughts even when I'm far away. [3]You see me when I travel and when I rest at home. You know everything I do. [4]You know what I am going to say even before I say it, LORD. [5]You go before me and follow me. You place your hand of blessing on my head. [6]Such knowledge is too wonderful for me, too great for me to understand! [7]I can never escape from your Spirit! I can never get away from your presence! [8]If I go up to heaven, you are there; if I go down to the grave, you are there. [9]If I ride the wings of the morning, if I dwell by the farthest oceans, [10]even there your hand will guide me, and your strength will support me. [11]I could ask the darkness to hide me and the light around me to become night—[12]but even in darkness I cannot hide from you. To you the night shines as bright as day. Darkness and light are the same to you.

These verses show how much God loves us—and nothing we think or do is hidden from Him. So why even try to hide things from Him, the One who loves us the most and can help us more than anyone else?

Like with Julia, God uses parents/guardians and mentors to help guide and protect those who are young. So isn't it foolish to hide things from the good authority figures in our lives? Is there anything in your life that you're hiding from parents/guardians/mentors? Explain your answers.

> Look back at the names you wrote down in the previous entry (of the adults you trust). Consider going to one of them and sharing what you wrote above.

> **Did you notice?**
>
> When Julia finally opened up and told John and Jenny about what had happened with Jay, she learned some things she hadn't previously known about her brother and his wife. She also discovered some things she'd failed to realize about herself.

Go back and re-read their conversation at the Cove. Write down things you learned about relationships or the way a man is wired:

GRAB YOUR JOURNAL and write about any time, like Julia, you've been really sad about something and found it hard to move on. How did you?

Chapter 3

Prince or Pauper?

✦ **WHEN JENNY** noticed that Julia was *still* acting sad (even after their talk at the Cove), she gave her some good advice. What did she say?

_____

_____

> **Proverbs 15:13 (NLT)**
> A glad heart makes a happy face; a broken heart crushes the spirit.

> **Proverbs 17:22 (NLT)**
> A cheerful heart is good medicine, but a broken spirit saps a person's strength.

> **TRUTH:** Feeling sorry for yourself won't help solve problems. However, **choosing joy** while you trust the Lord to resolve things, will give you strength to continue on, help heal your broken heart, and keep your spirit from being crushed.

Jenny's mom made up a story about *watching the clock*. What point was she trying to get across?

_____

_____

_____

How did you like Jenny's mother's interpretation of the Cinderella story? Which concepts were new to you or made you think differently?

_____

_____

_____

_____

Jenny's mom had said that while a girl may be anxious to be a bride, she may not be ready to become a wife. What did she mean? Do you agree with her?

_____

_____

_____

_____

_____

_____

_____

Before reading this chapter, had you ever thought about the fact that your future husband (assuming you want to be married one day) is somewhere right now, living life like you are? Does that motivate you to pray for him now? Why or why not?

_____

_____

_____

_____

_____

_____

_____

GRAB YOUR JOURNAL and write your thoughts on *Amy's glasses,* the story Julia shared.

Chapter 4

Beauty Lessons

✧ JULIA TOLD God she was seeing a dangerous pattern in her life. What was it?

_____
_____
_____
_____

Philippians 2:3-4 (NLT)
³Don't be selfish; don't try to impress others. Be humble, thinking of others as better than yourselves. ⁴Don't look out only for your own interests, but take an interest in others, too.

Cassie was a good example of this kind of unselfishness. Instead of dating Brian to impress her friends, she was exercising wisdom, thinking long-term, and trying to protect Brian's interests—putting them ahead of her own.

Can you think of a time when you put the interests of others ahead of your own? What happened?

_____
_____
_____
_____
_____
_____
_____
_____
_____

After reading several verses in Proverbs 31, Julia detected a flaw in her own heart—vanity. She was learning that God's Word is like a mirror into the soul. She wrote about what she was seeing as a prayer in her new journal, entering into an intimacy with God she had never experienced before.

> **Hebrews 4:12 (NLT)**
> For the word of God is alive and powerful. It is sharper than the sharpest two-edged sword, cutting between soul and spirit, between joint and marrow. It exposes our innermost thoughts and desires.

Has the Bible ever been a *mirror to your soul* when you were reading it? Explain.

_____
_____
_____
_____

Julia's mother taught her some important beauty lessons in this chapter. Go back and review them again. Write down two or three of her points. Did they cause you to see beauty (or even yourself) any differently? Explain.

_____
_____
_____
_____
_____
_____

GRAB YOUR JOURNAL and write to your Heavenly Father about how you feel about yourself these days, inside and out.

Chapter 5

No More Secrets

❖ JULIA GREW up never knowing the truth about her dad and his father. Phil was ashamed of his father and his own hatred of him, so he made Julia think that everything had been just fine. The deception he sowed by doing that reproduced years later—when Julia deceived him about her secret life at Tyler.

Proverbs 16:18 (NLT)	**Galatians 6:7 (CEV)**
Pride goes before destruction and haughtiness before a fall.	You cannot fool God, so don't make a fool of yourself! You will harvest what you plant.

It's important to know…

Pride often leads us to plant dishonest seeds in our lives. *The truth* puts us back on track. Yes, our pride may be hurt when we admit the truth, but the rewards that come from obeying God are always worth it!

Have you ever had to swallow your pride and admit the truth? What happened?

_____

_____

_____

_____

_____

_____

_____

_____

Julia learned some surprising things about her parents' courtship. Grace's father had stopped her from dating Phil until he could mentor him first. Grace wisely accepted her father's decision.

> **Proverbs 1:8 (NLT)**
> My child, listen when your father corrects you. Don't neglect your mother's instruction.

What did you think of Julia's grandfather? What did he see about Phil that his daughter Grace did not? Are *you* willing to listen to what your parents/guardians have to say about your relationships?

_____
_____
_____
_____
_____
_____
_____

How do you think things would have played out had Grace ignored her father's decision and dated Phil anyway?

_____
_____
_____
_____
_____
_____
_____

GRAB YOUR JOURNAL and write what you think you would do if you were in college, met a guy you were really attracted to, and then your parents/guardians said it wasn't a good idea to date him.

Chapter 6

Common Sense

✧ **WHEN JULIA** first started her job at the Center, she initially had trouble working in that environment. Why?

_____

_____

_____

_____

Have you ever visited someone (possibly a grandparent) in a nursing home? If so, what did you see and feel while you were there?

_____

_____

_____

_____

_____

Leviticus 19:32 (NIV)	**Job 12:12 (NIV)**
"'Stand up in the presence of the aged, show respect for the elderly and revere your God. I am the LORD.'"	Is not wisdom found among the aged? Does not long life bring understanding?

More than just a job...

As Julia got to know Miss Lottie and cared for the people at the Center, she took an interest in them and earned about their lives. She respected them and allowed their years of experience to teach her valuable lessons.

When Sophia was offered the chance to come to America and marry a stranger, she quickly agreed. Why? What do you think *you* would have done?

_____
_____
_____
_____
_____

Sophia said that girls today have an unrealistic, *Hollywood* view of marriage. What do *you* think and why?

_____
_____
_____
_____
_____

Sophia also said that her husband's looks didn't matter so much to her as long as he was a good and kind man. Would most girls today agree? Why or why not? Do you think the above question has anything to do with your answer?

_____
_____
_____
_____
_____

GRAB YOUR JOURNAL and write about any elderly people in your life. What have you learned from them?

Chapter 7

Sister Talk

❖ **JULIA WAS** angry and jealous when Keith decided to date another girl instead of her. Have you ever been jealous of another girl? Explain.

_____
_____
_____
_____

> Is it always wrong to be jealous?
> Did you know there is more than one way to be jealous?

Deuteronomy 32:15-16 (NLT)
¹⁵"But Israel soon became fat and unruly; the people grew heavy, plump, and stuffed! Then they abandoned the God who had made them; they made light of the Rock of their salvation. ¹⁶They stirred up his **jealousy** by worshiping foreign gods; they provoked his fury with detestable deeds."

He's perfect.
When we stray from God, He knows we are headed for big trouble. His jealousy and anger are motivated by **His love for us** and **His desire to provide for and protect us, to protect our covenant relationship with Him.**

We're not perfect.
Since we are made in God's image, we have the ability to become angry and jealous as well. But instead of **selfless** motivation, our feelings come from selfish interests. When we want something or someone's attention for ourselves and don't get it, it's easy to become angry and jealous of those who do. This kind of anger and jealousy is unhealthy and can consume a person.

> **Proverbs 27:4 (NLT)**
> Anger is cruel, and wrath is like a flood, but jealousy is even more dangerous.

> Jealousy fades when we realize just how much God loves us. As God becomes the One we need and seek the most (for love, acceptance, and worth), we begin to realize there is no need to be jealous of others. Our Heavenly Father is taking good care of us (*and* the desires of our hearts).

Could you identify with Julia's pain when Keith chose someone else over her? Elaborate.

_____
_____
_____
_____
_____
_____
_____

When Julia couldn't shake her anger and jealousy towards Keith, she turned to God for answers. He prompted her to talk with Jenny (since He knew she had been through something similar). When you are going through a tough time, does it help to know others have experienced similar things and were able to work through them? Why or why not?

_____
_____
_____
_____
_____

GRAB YOUR JOURNAL and write what you think of the following statement: *Sometimes man's rejection is actually God's protection.*

Chapter 8

Unwanted Admirer

✦   **WHEN JULIA** realized Flip had a big-time crush on her, she could have been painfully blunt with him, crushing his spirit and maybe even discouraging him from going to church anymore. Instead, she was **gentle** with him and tried to downplay his attentions, hoping he would see on his own that she wasn't interested in him as a boyfriend. Even though her plan didn't work, her heart was right in trying to protect his feelings and spiritual growth.

> **Ephesians 4:2 (NLT)**
> Always be humble and gentle. Be patient with each other, making allowance for each other's faults because of your love.

> **1 Peter 3:4 (NLT)**
> You should clothe yourselves instead with the beauty that comes from within, the unfading beauty of a gentle and quiet spirit, which is so precious to God.

> In every relationship, there are times when the truth must be spoken (even if someone's feelings may be hurt). Flip didn't have the maturity to see Julia wasn't interested in dating him. In fact, he was so self-centered, he was becoming pretty obnoxious! Julia had to confront him with the truth for his good as well as hers.

> **Ephesians 4:15 (NLT)**
> Instead, we will speak the truth in love, growing in every way more and more like Christ, who is the head of his body, the church.

Overall, how do you think Julia handled Flip? Would you have done anything differently?

_____

_____

_____

_____

_____

_____

_____

Flip threatened to hurt himself if Julia refused to love him. What would you answer if a guy said that to *you*?

_____

_____

_____

_____

_____

Why did Julia say in her journal that she was *grateful* Keith hadn't asked her out? How does this relate to the statement you wrote about in your last journal entry *(about man's rejection sometimes being God's protection)*?

_____

_____

_____

_____

_____

_____

_____

GRAB YOUR JOURNAL and write a short prayer for your future Mr. Right, like Julia did.

Chapter 9

Tall Paul

✧ JULIA WAS still communicating with her friends from Tyler. Gretchen and Gary had gotten engaged, and Karen was in love, too. When others are already experiencing what we want and still don't have, it's easy to compare ourselves to them and fear it will never happen for us. However, Jesus left us with a gift to combat our fears:

> **John 14:27 (NLT)**
> "I am leaving you with a gift—peace of mind and heart. And the peace I give is a gift the world cannot give. So don't be troubled or afraid."

> When Julia heard about her friends from Tyler, her natural reaction was to envy them a little. But rather than giving in to emotions that would do nothing to change her situation, she chose to be happy for her friends.

> **1 Corinthians 13:4 (NIV)**
> Love is patient, love is kind. It does not envy, it does not boast, it is not proud.

> **Matthew 11:28 (AMP)**
> Come to Me, all you who labor and are heavy-laden and overburdened, and I will cause you to rest. [I will ease and relieve and refresh your souls.]

Can you think of a time when a friend got something that you were still hoping to receive yourself? How did you respond?

_____

_____

_____

_____

_____
_____
_____
_____

When you're feeling hurt or forgotten, where do you go to find comfort? Are those the best places? Explain.
_____
_____
_____
_____

In the previous chapter, Julia had asked God to give her a close guy friend to hang out with until her Mr. Right came along. Do you think that was a good idea? Why or why not?
_____
_____
_____
_____

When you read that Julia had decided to leave for Tipton in the middle of the night, did you think anything of it? Would you have felt comfortable leaving that late?
_____
_____
_____

GRAB YOUR JOURNAL and write about any areas of your life where you don't feel peace. Write down what is bothering you. Ask God to take care of every detail as you give each one over to Him. Let Jesus refresh your soul and give you the peace He promises.

Chapter 10

Daffy Dinah

❖ JULIA LEFT all alone in the middle of the night feeling she was doing the right thing. (Cassie needed her!) However, feelings alone shouldn't drive our actions. We need to think before we act.

> **Proverbs 2:11 (NLT)**
> Wise choices will watch over you. Understanding will keep you safe.

To make wise choices, discuss your decisions and plans with parents/guardians and mentors. They may point out something you hadn't considered.

As the man from the convenience store tried to run Julia off the road, she immediately cried out to God for help.

> **Psalm 141:1 (NLT)**
> O LORD, I am calling to you. Please hurry! Listen when I cry to you for help!

Never forget...
Always cry out to God when you are in trouble.

Julia's grandmother talks about a young woman named Dinah in the Bible. Read through that story in Genesis 24. How did Dinah's brothers avenge her honor? What points were made in Julia's conversation with her grandparents in the car on the way to Tipton?

_____
_____
_____
_____
_____
_____

Julia's grandfather said that her *motive* for getting to Cassie as soon as possible was good, but her *plan* wasn't. Have you ever felt that way about something you did? Explain.

_____

_____

_____

_____

Julia's grandfather also pointed out that if Julia had been hurt, raped, or even killed, her whole family would have had to live through that nightmare. Do you think most people think about that before they decide to do something? Explain your answer.

_____

_____

_____

_____

Little details like having your cell phone charged or remembering to let people know where you are going can become big issues in an emergency. (Julia learned this the hard way!) Stop and think if anything you're doing (or not doing) might put you at risk if something goes wrong. Changing the way you do things now might make a huge difference one day if, like Julia, you find yourself in trouble. Write down anything you can think of that you need to change.

_____

_____

_____

GRAB YOUR JOURNAL and write how you think Julia benefited from such a scary experience.

Chapter 11

Current Events

❖ **RETURNING HOME** from Tipton, Julia called Flip about fixing her car. She also made plans to have Cassie stay with her until her parents returned from Chile. **True friends** are needed in everyone's life, but they are not always easy to find.

> **Proverbs 18:24 (NLT)**
> There are "friends" who destroy each other, but a real friend sticks closer than a brother.

Think about *your* friends for a moment. Are they the positive, *stick close* kind or ones that (if you're honest) are negatively affecting your life in some way? Explain your answer.

_____

_____

_____

> **Matthew 10:16 (CEV)**
> I am sending you like lambs into a pack of wolves. So be as wise as snakes and as innocent as doves.

In this verse, Jesus warns that we are living in a world filled with dangerous people. We women must be very cautious and intentional regarding where we go and with whom. God wants us to be innocent but not naïve.

Julia totally misread Professor McNulty's interest in her. When he invited her to go for ice cream, he really had something more in mind. How do you think she handled the situation that night? What would you have done?

_____

_____

When Julia got tricked into going with Professor McNulty in his car, she silently prayed to her Heavenly Father for help. Have you ever had to do that? What happened?

Julia went directly to her parents about Professor McNulty. Why was that a better plan than handling the situation herself?

GRAB YOUR JOURNAL and write about any situation in your life right now where, like Julia, you need some help. Then share what you wrote with an adult you trust.

Chapter 12

S.O.S. Online

✧ **WHEN WE** make mistakes in life, we might be tempted to think God can no longer use us for His purposes. But it's just the opposite! God often calls upon us to share our failures—to explain how we received His comfort and forgiveness to continue on. This encourages others to do the same.

> **2 Corinthians 1:3-4 (NLT)**
> ³All praise to God, the Father of our Lord Jesus Christ. God is our merciful Father and the source of all comfort. ⁴ He comforts us in all our troubles so that we can comfort others. When they are troubled, we will be able to give them the same comfort God has given us.

Can you think of a time when sharing a mistake (and what you learned from it) helped someone else? Explain.

_____
_____
_____
_____
_____
_____
_____

Julia happily accepted when asked to lead a girls' group. She wanted to help others succeed where she had failed. Although telling her story was embarrassing, the girls were moved by her honesty and admired her for her courage.

> **Proverbs 29:23 (NLT)**
> Pride ends in humiliation, while humility brings honor.

At the retreat, Julia talked about the dangers of covering up mistakes—where that can lead. Re-read that section and recap what she said.

_____
_____
_____
_____
_____
_____

Have you ever covered up a mistake you made? What happened?

_____
_____
_____
_____
_____
_____

Julia said it was dangerous to listen to someone's story and think, *That would never happen to **me**.* Why would that kind of attitude be dangerous?

_____
_____
_____
_____
_____

GRAB YOUR JOURNAL and write about an experience someone else shared that encouraged you.

Chapter 13

Reaching Out

✦ JULIA AND her mother allowed God to use them to help Shelly, the girl who was battling bulimia.

> **Psalm 107:17-19 (NLT)**
> ¹⁷Some were fools; they rebelled and suffered for their sins. ¹⁸They couldn't stand the thought of food, and they were knocking on death's door. ¹⁹"LORD, help!" they cried in their trouble, and he saved them from their distress.

> One time we may be serving as God's helper, another time, *the one crying out for help.*

> **Psalm 139: 14 (CEV)**
> ...and I praise you because of the wonderful way you created me. Everything you do is marvelous! Of this I have no doubt.

> **1 Corinthians 6:19-20 (NIV)**
> ¹⁹Do you not know that your body is a temple of the Holy Spirit, who is in you, whom you have received from God? You are not your own; ²⁰you were bought at a price. Therefore honor God with your body.

Reading the verses above, why is it important not to mistreat or abuse your body?

_____
_____
_____
_____
_____
_____

> When Shelly began purging to be thin enough to impress a boy, she didn't mean to damage her body. But wanting someone or something *more than wanting to please God* will always take us down a painful road. Eating disorders are often about taking back control of one's life from others. God wants us to surrender the control of our lives *to Him*. When we do that, we'll be traveling down a Christ-centered road that brings true fulfillment.

Realize this…
Some of the things you think you can't live without today won't be nearly as important later. That which is **good and lasting** shouldn't require you to sacrifice your **purity, health, or safety**.

What did you think of Mrs. Emerson's reaction to her daughter's confession of having an eating disorder?

___

___

___

___

When Julia saw Shelly was hurt by her mom's reaction, she shared some things she learned through her own mess up at Tyler. One of the things Julia said was, "…my parents weren't vending machines, standing by to instantly hand out everything I needed. They were people with needs and feelings of their own." Does this help you to see your parents/guardians any differently? Explain.

___

___

___

___

GRAB YOUR JOURNAL and write to the Lord about how you view yourself. Ask Him to help you see the beautiful and valuable young woman He has created, to help you appreciate all your wonderful attributes. Lastly, ask Him to protect your heart and mind so you can resist the wrong thoughts that come to all of us.

Chapter 14

First Kiss

❖   **WHEN JULIA** sensed Paul was beginning to want more than friendship, she asked God about it. She wasn't sure of her own feelings and realized she needed wisdom to do the right thing.

> **James 1:5 (NIV)**
> If any of you lacks wisdom, you should ask God, who gives generously to all without finding fault, and it will be given to you.

> Having wisdom about a situation means **understanding the truth** and then knowing how to **take proper action**.

After talking with Paul, Julia realized she would have to give up living in Weston if she married him. For her, that was a price she didn't want to pay. But before making any decisions about Paul, she wanted to pray first. Maybe God had a different plan than she did.

> **Luke 14:28 (NLT)**
> "But don't begin until you count the cost. For who would begin construction of a building without first calculating the cost to see if there is enough money to finish it?"

Was there ever a time you wished you had gotten some advice (from God and others) before running ahead with your own plans? Explain.

_____
_____
_____
_____
_____
_____

Were you surprised when Paul kissed Julia? Were you even more surprised when she pushed away from his second kiss? Why or why not?

Julia discussed her feelings about Paul with her mother. Do you think talking to someone can help you see a situation more clearly? Explain.

At the time, did you think that Julia's concerns about Paul were serious enough to keep them from moving forward with their relationship? What do you think *you* would have done?

GRAB YOUR JOURNAL and write about any area you need wisdom in right now. Ask God for His wisdom and to whom you should go for good advice.

Chapter 15

Readjusting the Focus

✦ **BEFORE GOING** to bed, Julia prayed about what to do about Paul. The next morning, she had her answer. What was it? What did it mean?

_____

_____

_____

_____

Even though Julia would miss going places with Paul, she was sure she was doing the right thing by refusing to go out with him anymore. There is a godly joy that comes from doing what's right (even when it hurts).

Psalm 106:3 (NLT)
There is joy for those who deal justly with others and always do what is right.

Have you ever done what was right even though it hurt? Explain.

_____

_____

_____

_____

_____

_____

1 Corinthians 6:18 (NIV)
Flee from sexual immorality. All other sins a person commits are outside the body, but whoever sins sexually, sins against their own body.

God tells us to run from sexual immorality because He loves us and wants to protect us. He isn't trying to merely restrict us or spoil our fun. Justine Keller communicated the consequences of ignoring God's warning.

Re-read Justine Keller's response to Passionate Pink's questions. Write down your thoughts and any additional questions regarding what she said.

_____
_____
_____
_____
_____
_____
_____

The Bible tells us in 2 Corinthians 6:14 not to become *unequally yoked* (intimately involved) with unbelievers. Jeanie's decision to marry a man from a different religion led to an irreversible tragedy in her life. Discuss why she made that choice, what happened, and how you reacted to her story, *Lost Angel*.

_____
_____
_____
_____
_____
_____
_____

Julia and the other web group leaders all put unattractive pictures of themselves as teens on the website for the girls to view. Why? Would you have the confidence to do that? (Would they have had the confidence at your age?)

GRAB YOUR JOURNAL and answer the above questions.

Chapter 16

Risky Business

❖   IN THE post *Deadly Games,* Tina was secretly communicating with a guy online. Her mother had no idea what was going on (until it was too late).

Psalm 141:9 (NIV)
Keep me safe from the traps set by evildoers, from the snares they have laid for me.

When Tina deliberately hid her online conversations from her mom, she moved out from under God's protection (via her family) and walked into the enemy's carefully-designed trap.

Proverbs 14: 26-27 (CEV)
²⁶If you respect the LORD, you and your children have a strong fortress ²⁷and a life-giving fountain that keeps you safe from deadly traps.

It's so important to respect both God and your parents/guardians. They are there to help you avoid danger **before** it has a chance to overtake you.

So now that you've read Tina's story (which *is* true to life), consider the following questions: Do you friend people online that you don't know personally? Are you communicating with anyone online or by phone that your parents/guardians don't know about? Can you now see the danger in those things? Write your answers below:

_____
_____
_____
_____
_____
_____

Now let's look at Karleen's story. Tired of waiting to meet her guy, she tried to find someone on her own through a Christian chat room, sure this was a safe way to meet a godly man. Karleen learned firsthand the following truth about online relationships:

> When you're not spending time with a guy in person, it's harder to evaluate his true character. Spending time with him helps you see the man he really is.

> **Matthew 7:20 (NLT)**
> "Yes, just as you can identify a tree by its fruit, so you can identify people by their actions."

When Karleen shared that she and her fiancé (who she had only known for a few weeks) were thinking about eloping, her friend told her, *"Time is your friend…"* What do you think she meant?

GRAB YOUR JOURNAL and ask your Heavenly Father to help you stay safe online. Write down any ways you might be putting yourself at risk. Then commit to change what you're doing. You have no idea the trap from which you might be saving yourself down the road!

Chapter 17

Staying Strong

❖ **AFTER HER** big mess up with Jay at Tyler University, Julia was determined to spend time getting to know God better—to allow Jesus to become the most important and meaningful relationship in her life. She was doing that by reading her Bible, praying, and honestly pouring out her heart to God in her journal.

> **Psalm 73:28 (NLT)**
> But as for me, how good it is to be near God! I have made the Sovereign LORD my shelter, and I will tell everyone about the wonderful things you do.

> **Psalm 37: 4 (NIV)**
> Take delight in the LORD, and he will give you the desires of your heart.

Although Julia was periodically frustrated about not meeting her guy yet, she was continuing to trust in God's faithfulness to make it happen.

It's not always easy to keep trusting God when what you want is slow in coming. Can you relate to anything Julia said to God in her journal? Go back and re-read her entry at the beginning of the chapter before responding.

_____
_____
_____
_____
_____
_____
_____
_____

> **Psalm 37:5 (NLT)**
> Commit everything you do to the Lord. Trust him, and he will help you.

We need God's help to do the right thing (for our lives and for the lives of others). When Paul told Julia he loved her and pleaded with her to date him on the weekends, God helped her to stay strong and say *no*. Why would it be wrong to just date Paul on the weekends until her Mr. Right showed up? Were you hoping she would?

Are you trusting God for your life right now? Do you ever spend time worshipping, reading your Bible, or writing to God in a journal? Why or why not?

GRAB YOUR JOURNAL and write about any area in your life where you need to stay strong. Ask God (and others) to help you!

Chapter 18

Ups and Downs

✧   **BECAUSE JULIA** had told Paul for the *second* time she couldn't return his love, he was looking very downcast the next morning at church. Setting necessary boundaries in a relationship can be difficult, especially when you feel bad about hurting someone.

> **Romans 12:18 (NIV)**
> If it is possible, as far as it depends on you, live at peace with everyone.

We are not responsible for the way others react when we tell them the truth in love. If possible, however, we should try to maintain a peaceful relationship.

Is there anyone in your life you need to pursue peace with? Explain.

_____

_____

_____

> Being at peace with people does not mean you have to maintain unhealthy relationships or put up with inappropriate advances, like Julia experienced with Professor McNulty. It's wise to *avoid* situations that could put you in danger. When Julia bumped into the professor again in the hallway, he was as creepy and inappropriate as always, necessitating her speedy retreat down the east stairway!

> **Proverbs 14:16 (NLT)**
> The wise are cautious and avoid danger; fools plunge ahead with reckless confidence.

Have you ever been in a similar situation (with an adult that made you feel uncomfortable)? Julia shared what was going on with her parents so they could help walk her through it. *Have you told a trusted adult what happened and how you felt about it?* Please consider doing so. Like Julia, you will be glad you have someone else's wisdom and support.

> **1 Samuel 18:1 (CEV)**
> David and Saul finished talking, and soon David and Jonathan became best friends. Jonathan thought as much of David as he did of himself.

Julia and Cassie were as close as David and Jonathan. These young women shared a friendship that some people never find. When Brian and Cassie told Julia they were engaged, how did she react in spite of the fact that she hadn't met her own Mr. Right yet? How would you have responded to Cassie's news had you been in Julia's position?

_____

_____

_____

_____

_____

> Julia decided *not* to go to the singles' New Year's Eve party. She knew as lonely and frustrated as she was feeling, she might run into Paul's arms the moment she saw him. Maybe she'd even agree to marry him in such a weak moment! No, it was safer to stay home that night.

> **1 Corinthians 10:13 (NLT)**
> The temptations in your life are no different from what others experience. And God is faithful. He will not allow the temptation to be more than you can stand. When you are tempted, he will show you a way out so that you can endure.

As strong as Julia had been up to this point, what does this tell you about the potential for all of us to have weak moments? What does it also say about knowing your limitations and not putting yourself in tempting situations? How does the above verse encourage you?

GRAB YOUR JOURNAL and answer the above questions.

Chapter 19

Internal Affairs

✦   **O**UT OF love and concern for others, Jolene Ashton shared her story with the web group. For years, she had been trapped in a cycle of abuse and shame at home.

> **John 8:32 (AMP)**
> And you will know the Truth, and the Truth will set you free.

> **Psalm 142:7 (CEV)**
> Rescue me from this prison, so I can praise your name. And when your people notice your wonderful kindness to me, they will rush to my side.

> It wasn't until Jolene heard the truth about God's love for her that she received the courage to *tell the truth about what was happening*. Once she asked the Lord for help (and did what she felt He told her), people were able to rescue her and find loving parents for her. Now He was drawing people to her side to hear her testimony about His wonderful kindness.

Is there anything in your life that feels like a prison? Are there things you know you need to share with someone? Below, write down the names of two adults you trust to help you work through your "stuff" in life. (I know we've done this before, but it's a good reminder of who is there for you!) Then pray and ask God for the courage to communicate the details of your situation, whatever it may be, to one of the people below.

_____

_____

> **Ephesians 6:1-3 (NLT)**
> ¹Children, obey your parents because you belong to the Lord, for this is the right thing to do. ²"Honor your father and mother." This is the first commandment with a promise: ³If you honor your father and mother, "things will go well for you, and you will have a long life of the earth."

> We've already discussed earlier in this workbook the necessity and great benefit of obeying parents. Even so, we need to emphasize again that *obeying parents does not mean submitting to abuse.* Children are to obey when what the parents require from them does not contradict Scripture. If you or someone you know is experiencing true abuse at home, it's important that you speak up to a trusted adult to get help. As Jolene said, *Silence is the abuser's only protection.* The truth must be known for change to happen.

When Taffy Cream wrote to the web group about abuse in her home, Jolene investigated the situation and found it wasn't really abuse, just poor communication between Taffy Cream and her parents regarding friends and privileges. Re-read Jolene's post to Taffy Cream and jot down any lines that jump out at you. Also write your thoughts on the following statements: *There's never going to be a time in your life when you can just do whatever you want without regard for anyone else. You're always going to have to answer to somebody else's rules...*

_____
_____
_____
_____
_____

*In this stage of life, Julia was **doing good**—making a great impact in her ministry with the girls at church. At the same time, she was getting **faint-hearted** regarding what she was believing for personally.*

> **Galatians 6:9 (NKJV)**
> And let us not grow weary while doing good, for in due season we shall reap if we do not lose heart.

Julia poured out her frustrations to God about not meeting her Mr. Right yet. Review what she wrote in her journal entry. What did Julia mean by not wanting her desire for a boyfriend to become an idol?

GRAB YOUR JOURNAL and answer the above question. Also write about any ways you might feel weary right now. Don't lose heart! Instead, pour out your feelings to the Lord like Julia did. He'll help you hang in there and reap good things in due season as you continue to trust Him.

Chapter 20

Déjà Vu

❖   **BEFORE GOING** to the hospital, Julia had committed to trust the Lord completely for the time and place to meet her guy. Knowing that God was both able and *willing* to make it happen, she took control of her emotions and *chose to be at peace* until it did happen. Her only responsibility was to faithfully serve Him by serving others while she waited. (Yes, easier said than done, but true all the same!)

> **Psalm 37:5 (AMP)**
> Commit your way to the Lord [roll and repose each care of your load on Him]; trust (lean on, rely on, and be confident) also in Him and He will bring it to pass.

> Julia could trust God to bring her together with the right man at the right time because she already knew *His will* in the matter when she prayed, and He never lies (fails to keep His promises).

> **Genesis 2:18 (NLT)**
> Then the LORD God said, "It is not good for the man to be alone. I will make a helper who is just right for him."
>
> **1 John 5:14-15 (NIV)**
> [14]This is the confidence we have in approaching God: that if we ask anything according to his will, he hears us. [15]And if we know that he hears us—whatever we ask—we know that we have what we asked of him.
>
> **Numbers 23:19 (CEV)**
> God is no mere human! He doesn't tell lies or change his mind. God always keeps his promises.

What do the above verses mean to you?

_____

_____

___

___

___

Would it surprise you to know that the moment you pray in faith for something **in line with God's will,** your prayer is immediately answered? You may not see it happen right away, but God is working behind the scenes ensuring its timely arrival.

> **Isaiah 65:24 (CEV)**
> I will answer their prayers before they finish praying.

Speaking of timely arrival, what did you think of David (and his rescue of Julia from McNulty)?

___

___

___

> **Psalm 91:4b, 14-16 (NLT)**
> ⁴...His faithful promises are your armor and protection.
>
> ¹⁴The Lord says, "I will rescue those who love me. I will protect those who trust in my name. ¹⁵When they call on me, I will answer; I will be with them in trouble. I will rescue and honor them. ¹⁶I will reward them with a long life and give them my salvation."

> **Psalm 140:1-2a (NKJV)**
> ¹Deliever me, Oh Lord, from evil men; preserve me from violent men, who plan evil things in their hearts...

> Obviously, we must make the best decisions we can regarding our safety, but it's comforting to know that God is watching out for us, ready to rescue and deliver, as Julia found out in that parking lot.

GRAB YOUR JOURNAL and write what you thought of the novel's ending. Also, write out a prayer asking God to protect you and keep you safe at all times.

Novel 3

Chapter 1

The Shortcut

❖ **AS NOVEL** three begins, Julia is just days away from her wedding. Did that surprise you? Did you like the novel beginning this way? Describe your thoughts on the accident starting off the plot.

_____
_____
_____
_____
_____
_____
_____

Did you think Julia was foolish to take an unfamiliar shortcut to outrun that storm? Why or why not?

_____
_____
_____
_____
_____

By this point, Julia has learned to go to God with everything—big and small. Since the Lord already knows what we're going through, why do you think He still wants us to talk to Him about it all?

_____
_____
_____
_____

> **James 1:2-4 (NLT)**
> ²Dear brothers and sisters, when troubles come your way, consider it an opportunity for great joy. ³For you know that when your faith is tested, your endurance has a chance to grow. ⁴So let it grow, for when your endurance is fully developed, you will be perfect and complete, needing nothing.

Julia left the cottage for home, her day going perfectly, just as planned. Her faith, however, was about to be tested in ways she had never imagined. Has your faith ever been tested? Explain your situation and what you gained by going through it.

_____

_____

_____

_____

_____

_____

Getting her grandfather's watch fixed for David meant a lot to Julia; she trusted God to help her find a way. When He did, she was very grateful and remembered to sincerely thank Him.

> **Colossians 2:7 (NLT)**
> Let your roots grow down into him, and let your lives be built on him. Then your faith will grow strong in the truth you were taught, and you will overflow with thankfulness.

> Take a minute and think about your own heart. Is it overflowing with thankfulness for the good areas of your life?

GRAB YOUR JOURNAL and write down 5-10 things you can thank God for today.

Chapter 2

No Answer

❖ JULIA REACTED after her accident like most of us would have. Fortunately, her panic and tears eventually gave way to her trust in God's ability and willingness to help her. The years she had spent developing a close relationship with God (and learning what His Word promised her), *strengthened Julia's faith* to believe for the best in an almost hopeless situation. Did her prayer in this chapter inspire you? Which lines really stood out to you?

_____

_____

_____

_____

Deuteronomy 31:8 (AMP)
It is the Lord Who goes before you; He will [march] with you; He will not fail you or let you go or forsake you; [let there be no cowardice or flinching, but] fear not, neither become broken [in spirit depressed, dismayed, and unnerved with alarm].

2 Timothy 1:7 (NKJV)
For God has not given us a spirit of fear, but of power and of love and of a sound mind.

Hebrews 11:1 (NLT)
Faith is the confidence that what we hope for will actually happen; it gives us assurance about things we cannot see.

Fear weakens faith, so it must be dealt with so we can continue to trust God to fulfill His promises. The verse above says the Lord has not given us a spirit of fear. So when fear comes, as it often will in life, we have to take it to the Father so He can replace it with what we need (power, love, and a healthy mind or perspective).

> Quoting Scriptures (like Julia did) is a great way to drive fear away and replace wrong thoughts with right ones. *The thoughts we focus on make all the difference!*

Proverbs 4:23 (CEV)
Carefully guard your thoughts…

Psalm 19:14 (CEV)
Let my words and my thoughts be pleasing to you, Lord, because you are my rock and my protector.

Isaiah 26:3 (NLT)
You will keep in perfect peace all who trust in you, all whose thoughts are fixed on you!

Philippians 4:6-7 (NLT)
⁶Don't worry about anything; instead, pray about everything. Tell God what you need, and thank Him for all he has done. ⁷Then you will experience God's peace, which exceeds anything we can understand. His peace will guard your hearts and minds as you live in Christ Jesus.

Philippians 4:8 (CEV)
Finally, my friends, keep your minds on whatever is true, pure, right, holy, friendly, and proper. Don't ever stop thinking about what is truly worthwhile and worthy of praise.

Are you fighting fear or worry about anything today? Explain.

_____
_____
_____
_____
_____

GRAB YOUR JOURNAL and write a prayer to God, giving all your worries to Him and asking for a peace that will guard your heart and mind.

Chapter 3

No Fairy Tale

❖ **Tired of** trying to stay optimistic while waiting to be rescued, Julia relaxed and began to mentally relive her love story with David. Why did she say meeting David was so similar to when she had met Jay years before?

After picking up her car at the hospital, Julia heard God ask her to pray for Professor McNulty. Why did He want her to do that? Naturally, she was still upset about what that man had done to her and didn't feel like praying for him! *Why did she do it anyway?*

> **Matthew 5:44 (CEV)**
> But I tell you to love your enemies and pray for anyone who mistreats you.
>
> **Romans 12:19 (CEV)**
> Dear friends, don't try to get even. Let God take revenge. In the Scriptures the Lord says, "I am the one to take revenge and pay them back."

> As Christians, we are asked to be a witness of God's goodness to others. He alone knows a person's heart, their motives for doing things. Because He is LORD of all, He reserves the exclusive right to judge all things.

Even though Julia had chosen to forgive McNulty, he still had to be held accountable for what he had done in order to protect other young women. What did you think of the scene in the university president's office? Did it surprise you when McNulty accused Julia of being the problem? What did you think of how David defended Julia?

_____
_____
_____
_____
_____
_____
_____
_____

At the very end of this chapter, Julia gives a really good reason for forgiving. What was it? Do you agree or disagree? Why?

_____
_____
_____
_____
_____

Is there anyone you need to forgive in prayer *(whether you feel like it or not)?*

GRAB YOUR JOURNAL and write to the Lord about that last question.

Chapter 4

Sending Daisies

❖ **BECAUSE JULIA** loved God and wanted to please Him, she did her best to ignore Paul's rude behavior toward David, even though it irritated her greatly. Do you find it hard to keep quiet when someone's behavior is irritating? Explain.

_____
_____
_____
_____

Psalm 19:14 (NLT)
May the words of my mouth and the meditation of my heart be pleasing to you, O Lord, my rock and my redeemer.

Ephesians 4:2 (NLT)
Always be humble and gentle. Be patient with each other, making allowance for each other's faults because of your love.

Julia had learned that relationships need to be tested with time. Her haste in the past had caused her a lot of unnecessary pain. Knowing that, she was moving slowly with David.

Proverbs 19:2 (NLT)
Enthusiasm without knowledge is no good; haste makes mistakes.

Write about a time when rushing into something (without thinking or praying first) turned out to be a mistake.

_____
_____
_____
_____

After lunch, David asked to pay for Julia's meal. Why did she find that so refreshing?

Why do you think David sent Julia daisies instead of roses? Why was Julia glad he did?

Write down one thing you liked about David (his character) from this chapter and why.

GRAB YOUR JOURNAL and ask God to help you always think things through before rushing into something you may regret.

Chapter 5

A Cinderella Story

✦ **EVEN THOUGH** Julia *was* attracted to David, his friendship seemed more important to her than romance at this stage in their relationship. Why?

_____

_____

_____

_____

_____

Song of Solomon 5:16 (AMP)	Song of Solomon 2:7 (NLT)
His voice and speech are exceedingly sweet; yes, he is altogether lovely [the whole of him delights and is precious]. This is my beloved, and this is my friend, O daughters of Jerusalem!	Promise me, O women of Jerusalem...not to awaken love until the time is right.

Do you want to be married someday?
Then consider the following advice...

Ask God for a Christian man with spiritual maturity, one you can enjoy talking with, who delights your heart to be around, who has similar interests and goals and will make a suitable lifetime partner for you in marriage. Don't worry; if God is allowed to select him, you *will* be attracted to each other, and romance will be in the mix—just not the only ingredient. Your job is to trust God to make love happen *when He feels you're ready.* Be patient. (It's not always easy, but definitely worth the wait.)

> **Genesis 2:18 (CEV)**
> The LORD God said, "It isn't good for the man to live alone. I need to make a suitable partner for him."

When you understand that God is developing you into a suitable partner for your guy—and carefully selecting him just for you—it will make it easier to wait on His perfect timing!

List a few things you should be looking for in a relationship with a guy:

_____

_____

_____

When Julia started thinking about her relationship with David, she worriedly asked God if it was headed toward the same unhappy ending as her relationship with Paul. Julia found herself praying, *Lord, please help me not to worry about things that may never happen. Help me to enjoy the good of today and trust you for my tomorrow.* What are your thoughts on those last two sentences?

_____

_____

_____

Cassie showed up at Julia's house upset that the place where they had booked their wedding reception had just burned down. There were no other openings for their wedding date at any of the reception halls in the area, except for the country club, which was way out of her price range. How did Julia's parents solve her problem? Julia's mom said that Cassie played a part in finding that solution. What was it?

_____

_____

_____

GRAB YOUR JOURNAL and write to the Lord about the Mr. Right you are hoping to marry one day (or any other dream you may have).

Chapter 6

The Other Woman

♦ **JULIA STARTED** out her day happy about her relationship with David. That all changed when she called to thank him for her daisies. When David referred to his running partner as a *she*, did you think there was another woman there with him, too? How could Julia have handled that phone call better? What would *you* have said?

_____

_____

_____

_____

_____

_____

_____

*Julia was quick to believe the worst about David. Why? It's possible that having been **repeatedly deceived by Jay**, she was subconsciously afraid to fully trust a guy again. Like we said earlier, it is important to bring our fears to God and let Him help us overcome them.*

Job 3:25 (NIV)
What I feared has come upon me; what I dreaded has happened to me.

Often past hurts or disappointments make people afraid that the same heartbreaking things will happen again. Due to this, it's easy for them to jump to conclusions before verifying the facts.

2 Corinthians 13:1 (CEV)
I am on my way to visit you for the third time. And as the Scriptures say, "Any charges must be proved true by at least two or three witnesses."

Have you ever jumped to conclusions before getting all the facts? Explain what happened.

Sensing why Julia had hung up so abruptly, David set out to find her right away and straighten things out. Did you like the way he handled the misunderstanding? Explain your answer.

Were you surprised David's running partner was his dog, or had you already figured it out?

GRAB YOUR JOURNAL and write about being a friend who chooses to believe the best of others.

Chapter 7

Dinner and a Movie

❖ **WHEN JULIA** walked out of work, David pulled up in his car and handed her something through his window. What was it? Why did it make Julia's mother smile when she saw it later?

_____
_____
_____
_____
_____

Isaiah 43:18-19 (NIV)
18"Forget the former things; do not dwell on the past. 19See, I am doing a new thing! Now it springs up; do you not perceive it? I am making a way in the wilderness and streams in the wasteland.

For years, Julia had prayed and believed that God would send just the right man to love her. As she waited, it often felt like she was in a romantic wasteland, with no prospects in sight. Now that love was starting to bloom for her with David, she was ready to let go of the past, relax, and enjoy the ride!

Is there anything from your past you need to let go of, so you can receive the new thing God wants to do in and for you? Does Julia's story remind you how important it is to *keep trusting God*, even when it feels like the answer to your prayers is nowhere in sight? Explain your answers.

_____
_____
_____
_____
_____

David explained to Julia at dinner how and why he had come to Weston to set up his practice. As she listened to him, she realized that being a doctor was more than his career choice; it was a divine call to help the sick and suffering find lasting healing and wholeness.

> **Matthew 14:14 (AMP)**
> When He went ashore and saw a great throng of people, He had compassion (pity and deep sympathy) for them and cured their sick.

What touched David's heart his first time at a seminar by Dr. Feinberg? Why?

What pulls at your heart? What stirs compassion in you?

GRAB YOUR JOURNAL and ask God how to put your compassion to His use.

Chapter 8

A Happier Melody

❖ **IN THE** opening of this chapter, David and Paul had yet another unfriendly exchange. Review it again. Did you like how David handled Paul? Why or why not?

_____

_____

_____

_____

_____

When he was called away during the service, Paul took advantage of David's absence and asked Julia out to lunch after church. Pulling Paul to a private place, Julia took this opportunity to confront him face to face about his behavior.

> **Galatians 2:11 (NLT)**
> But when Peter came to Antioch, I had to oppose him to his face, for what he did was very wrong.

There are times when it's necessary to confront others about their behavior. Julia told Paul that the way he treated David had proven something to her. What was it? What would *you* have said to Paul about the way he was acting?

_____

_____

_____

_____

When Melody began acting uneasy around her, Julia prayed for God's help before saying anything. When a good opportunity came, Julia lovingly confronted Melody. As the truth came out, their friendship was restored.

> **Proverbs 18:19 (CEV)**
> Making up with a friend you have offended is harder than breaking through a city wall.
>
> **John 8:32 (NIV)**
> "Then you will know the truth, and the truth will set you free."

> It can feel awkward talking through misunderstandings or hurt feelings between friends. A lot of people skip the effort it takes to get things right. Some people move on to new friends. Others stay in the friendship, burying hurts and offenses that will no doubt eventually surface again, one way or another. Genuine friends will endure the awkwardness to work things out and keep the friendship honest and healthy.

Is talking with friends like this easy or hard for you? Explain.

_____
_____
_____
_____
_____
_____

In this chapter God answered one of Julia's prayers about Paul. Which one?

_____
_____
_____

GRAB YOUR JOURNAL and ask God to make you a friend who can work through uncomfortable situations.

Chapter 9

Tradition

✦ **WHILE HELPING** her mother prepare the food for Cassie's shower, Julia explained that she was trying to pay more attention when her mom was cooking. Why?

_____
_____
_____
_____

Now that David was in her life, Julia wanted to prepare her heart and skills to be a virtuous and capable wife—secretly hoping David might be her guy.

Proverbs 31:10-12 (NLT)
[10]Who can find a virtuous and capable wife? She is more precious than rubies. [11]Her husband can trust her, and she will greatly enrich his life. [12]She brings him good, not harm, all the days of her life.

The above verses praise the woman who proves to be a good wife. Her worth in God's Kingdom and to her husband is so great, it cannot be measured.

According to Scripture, the spiritually mature, older women of the church are supposed to train the younger women to truly love their families and maintain well-run, godly Christian homes.

Titus 2:3-5 (NLT)
[3]Similarly, teach the older women to live in a way that honors God. They must not slander others or be heavy drinkers. Instead, they should teach others what is good. [4]These older women must train the younger women to love their husbands and their children, [5]to live wisely and be pure, to work in their homes, to do good, and to be submissive to their husbands. Then they will not bring shame on the word of God.

Below, share any lines that impacted you from Julia's grandmother's message at the ladies' meeting. The main topics are given below:

Give and take in marriage:
_____
_____
_____

Maintaining a well-run, peaceful home:
_____
_____
_____

Importance of sex in marriage to a man:
_____
_____
_____

Submission:
_____
_____
_____

What's most needed in a woman's heart/a man's heart:
_____
_____
_____

GRAB YOUR JOURNAL and continue writing there if you need more space.

Chapter 10

On the Terrace

✦ **AFTER CASSIE'S** shower, Julia invited her friend to spend the night. She had a special reason. What was it? Explain what they did.

_____
_____
_____
_____

At Tyler University, Julia learned that the wrong kind of friends can lead you into wrong choices, even turn you against your parents.

Proverbs 28:7 (NLT)
Young people who obey the law are wise; those with wild friends bring shame to their parents.

Cassie, however, had always been a faithful and caring friend—one who brought out the best in Julia. These are the friends we should always **seek and keep!**

Proverbs 27:17 (CEV)
Just as iron sharpens iron, friends sharpen the minds of each other.

So, into what category do *your* friends fall? Are they ones who bring out the best in you? Or do they lead you in wrong directions? Explain your answers.

_____
_____
_____
_____
_____
_____

> **Romans 12:14 (AMP)**
> Bless those who persecute you [who are cruel in their attitude toward you]; bless and do not curse them.

Although Julia was tired of Paul's persistently annoying behavior toward her and David, she showed spiritual maturity by the way she refused to speak spitefully to Paul. Instead, she prayed for him to leave the area and trusted God to make it happen.

Take a minute and think about your conversations lately. Are they blessing those who give you a hard time? Do you pray for those people? Why do you think God expects us to bless (instead of tear down) those who seem against us?

_____
_____
_____
_____
_____

Did you enjoy watching David rescue Julia from Paul at Cassie's wedding? Did you feel sorry for Paul at all? Explain why or why not.

_____
_____
_____
_____
_____
_____
_____
_____

GRAB YOUR JOURNAL and write a prayer of blessing over someone whose attitude toward you isn't right. Ask God to help you see that person the way He does.

Chapter 11

Flight 459

❖ **JULIA'S FAMILY** had a dress code for Sunday morning services. Julia explained it wasn't for any spiritual reasons, just because her dad liked it that way. How did Julia respond to her dad's request that she wear skirts and dresses on Sundays? Why? How did David fit in with her dad's preference?

_____
_____
_____
_____
_____

When David invited Julia to have lunch with him at the park, she wanted to do more than just eat with him; she wanted to do something for him. **Genuine love is willing to inconvenience self in order to be a blessing to someone else.** *This is the key to real happiness.*

> **Philippians 2:4 (NKJV)**
> Let each of you look out not only for his own interests, but also for the interests of others.

The more we do for others, the more fulfilled we are. And God will remember our giving to others, rewarding us by making what we hope for come true.

> **Hebrews 6:10-11 (NLT)**
> ¹⁰For God is not unjust. He will not forget how hard you have worked for him and how you have shown your love to him by caring for other believers, as you still do. ¹¹Our great desire is that you will keep on loving others as long as life lasts, in order to make certain that what you hope for will come true.

Can you remember a time when doing something nice for someone else blessed *you* just as much? Explain.

_____
_____
_____
_____
_____

What was the surprise Julia's grandfather announced at a family dinner one night?

_____
_____

When John and Jenny returned from Chile, they brought with them their new daughter, the little girl they had adopted from an orphanage there. What secret did little Magda's shirt reveal?

_____
_____

Jenny and John were so excited to be able to adopt little Magda into their family. Are you adopted, or do you know anyone who is? Have you ever thought about the fact that adoption can *completely change someone's life*, their destiny, so to speak? Are you willing to open your heart to the possibility of adopting a child someday, if God brought the opportunity? Obviously, this isn't a realistic option now if you are a teen, but there are lots of ways to sponsor a child in your country or around the world, if that's something that interests you. It could even be something you do with your family or a group of committed friends. Pray and ask God if this is something He wants you to do at some point in your life.

GRAB YOUR JOURNAL and write down your thoughts on the above paragraph.

Chapter 12

The Letter

❖ **JULIA AWAKES** in this chapter feeling the arms of contentment embracing her. Why?

_____
_____
_____

Waiting so long to have a guy in her life had caused Julia's heart to become discouraged. Now David's friendship was fulfilling that longing. Each morning arrived with great expectations of what might be.

Proverbs 13:12 (NIV)
Hope deferred makes the heart sick, but a longing fulfilled is a tree of life.

Often in life, we're so focused on what we *don't* have, what *hasn't* happened yet, we forget to be encouraged by the prayers and desires God *has* answered! We forget to let those things be *trees of life* to us, refreshing our soul as we recognize that God loves us and takes good care of us. Gratitude is powerful! It can usher in peace and contentment for today, plus confidence that *your Heavenly Father will take care of tomorrow.*

As Julia watched David relate with her little niece Magda, she learned two things about him. What were they, and which was the most important to Julia? Is that important to you with your Mr. Right someday? List other things that are important to you regarding your future Mr. Right.

_____
_____
_____
_____

Things seemed to be going perfectly between Julia and David until his attitude toward her suddenly changed overnight. Remembering her past mistake, Julia didn't immediately confront David. She chose to think the best of him instead, even though she had received a disturbing email from Paul about David.

> **Proverbs 18:13 (NLT)**
> Spouting off before listening to the facts is both shameful and foolish.

Have you ever gone off on someone without knowing all the facts? Has anyone ever done that to you? Explain what happened.

When you were reading this chapter, why did you think David was acting so strangely? Were you as surprised as Julia about Paul's letter or had you figured out Paul was somehow to blame for the misunderstanding? Explain.

GRAB YOUR JOURNAL and write down as many answered prayers and "longings fulfilled" as you can think of, big and small. Let each one be a tree of life for you, reminding you of God's goodness and faithfulness, giving you a shaded place to rest from the heat of current challenges.

Chapter 13

A First

❖ **How did** Julia manage to reserve a table at Celestial Gardens on a night when they weren't taking reservations?

_____
_____
_____

> Sometimes, things don't seem to be working out the way we want. But if we continue to trust God, He can provide solutions in ways we hadn't thought of on our own.

After asking David to meet her at Celestial Gardens, Julia began getting ready for the evening, trusting God to help her explain what had happened.

> **Proverbs 16:1 (NIV)**
> To humans belong the plans of the heart, but from the LORD comes the proper answer of the tongue.

Have you ever been in a situation where you needed God to give you the right words? Explain what happened.

_____
_____
_____
_____
_____
_____
_____

> **2 John 1:12 (NLT)**
> I have much more to say to you, but I don't want to do it with paper and ink. For I hope to visit you soon and talk with you face to face. Then our joy will be complete.

Julia and David talked everything out over dinner, what each one was thinking and feeling over the last two weeks, why they had acted the way they did. Communication is a beautiful thing! Think of how quickly things would have been resolved had they swallowed their pride and talked this out in person right away. Notice it works better in person. Sometimes a text, email, or even phone call can be misunderstood. But when you're sitting across from each other, you can read each other's expressions and better understand what's really being said.

> **Song of Solomon 1:2 (CEV)**
> Kiss me tenderly! Your love is better than wine...

God created romantic love, not Hollywood. All kisses are not alike. **True love's kisses** *are well worth waiting for. All others are mere imitations.*

It is in this chapter where Julia received her first kiss from David. Where were they at the time, and what did he give her to always remember it?

_____

_____

_____

_____

Julia and David wisely trusted God to awaken love when the timing was right for both of them.

> **Song of Solomon 2:7 (NLT)**
> Promise me, O women of Jerusalem by the gazelles and wild deer, not to awaken love until the time is right.

GRAB YOUR JOURNAL and ask the Lord to help you wait for His timing for romance.

Chapter 14

The Real Thing

❖ **WHEN JULIA'S** alarm went off, she was excited to go downstairs and tell her parents all about her date with David. Her parents had something to tell her about a recent meeting David had arranged with her father. What was that all about?

_____

_____

_____

_____

Why had Julia and Cassie written a story for the youth group girls about how to dress? Did you agree or disagree with what Julia's grandparents said about dress?

_____

_____

_____

_____

*Have you noticed that throughout this series, most of the chapters end in the evening with Julia going to bed, reflecting on her day, with the next chapter beginning the next morning? That's real life! Each day begins with potential blessings and challenges ahead. Our trust (or lack of trust) in God **and** our moment-by-moment decisions will affect what we experience each day.*

> **Lamentations 3:22-23 (NLT)**
> ²²The faithful love of the LORD never ends! His mercies never cease. ²³Great is his faithfulness; his mercies begin afresh each morning.

Do you take time to reflect on your day while lying in bed at night? When do you make time in your schedule for prayer?

Ephesians 4:30-32 (NLT)
[30]And do not bring sorrow to God's Holy Spirit by the way you live. Remember, he has identified you as his own, guaranteeing that you will be saved on the day of redemption. [31]Get rid of all bitterness, rage, anger, harsh words, and slander, as well as all types of evil behavior. [32]Instead, be kind to each other, tenderhearted, forgiving one another, just as God through Christ has forgiven you.

Mark 11:25 (AMP)
And whenever you stand praying, if you have anything against anyone, forgive him *and* let it drop (leave it, let it go), in order that your Father Who is in heaven may also forgive you your (own) failings *and* shortcomings *and* let them drop.

Why do you think God asks us to release grudges and forgive?

Even though Julia and David were still angry with Paul, they chose to forgive him, asking God to forgive him as well. David said that if they waited until they felt like it, they might never do it. Remembering how gracious God has been to forgive all of *our* sins (past, present and future), should prompt us to forgive others when they sin against us. If we refuse, we bring sorrow to the Holy Spirit and allow our refusal to forgive to slowly poison us.

GRAB YOUR JOURNAL and write out a prayer thanking God for forgiving your sins and "letting them drop." Ask for His grace and strength to do the same for others.

Chapter 15

Think It Through

❖ **Now that** Julia and David had openly declared their love for each other, their relationship took on even more meaning—all the insecurities and guesswork behind them. Julia was thoroughly enjoying this season of her life. A belated surprise from David arrived in the beginning of this chapter. What was it? Were you expecting this to happen?

_____

_____

_____

_____

_____

While dating David, Julia submitted herself to her parents' authority and restrictions. Even Julia and David set up safeguards to keep themselves pure. They also associated with godly people who understood why having sex before marriage was wrong and supported their desire to avoid temptation.

> **2 Timothy 2:22 (CEV)**
> Run from temptations that capture young people. Always do the right thing. Be faithful, loving, and easy to get along with. Worship with people whose hearts are pure.

Consider the following:

If you do not intentionally make a plan to succeed, you most likely will not *(no matter what dream you have)*. A plan involves thinking through possible scenarios and preparing for them in advance, as much as possible. It also involves *sticking to your plan* (boundaries you have created, rules you've made for yourself), even when it's tempting to set it aside for a moment.

It takes *consistency* to experience lasting success. If you only stick to your convictions part of the time, unwanted problems are sure to follow.

Write down two of your most important dreams:

_____
_____

David took marriage very seriously. To him it was a lifetime covenant. That's why he wanted Julia to look past their present attraction for each other and decide if she would be able to handle the obvious sacrifices that being a doctor's wife would require.

> **Luke 14:28 (NKJV)**
> "For which of you, intending to build a tower, does not sit down first and count the cost, whether he has *enough* to finish *it*…"

Look at the two dreams you wrote above. Will you have to make any sacrifices to see them come true? Count the cost for a moment and list what things will be required of you to see those dreams realized. Are you willing to discipline yourself to do what it takes? Answer below.

_____
_____
_____
_____
_____
_____
_____
_____
_____
_____
_____

GRAB YOUR JOURNAL and write to God about your dreams. Ask Him to give you a practical plan for seeing your dreams come true, step by step.

Chapter 16

A Different Christmas

❖   **JULIA AND** David planned to spend Christmas Eve and Day with the Duncans and then drive to Baymont the following day to celebrate with David's parents. How did Julia feel about meeting them for the first time?

_____

_____

On Christmas Eve, Julia deliberately saved David's gift to open last, certain it was an engagement ring. When it was a bracelet she had admired instead, Julia hid her disappointment and graciously thanked David. She didn't want to hurt his feelings; they had become more important to her than her own.

> **Proverbs 16:24 (NIV)**
> Gracious words are a honeycomb, sweet to the soul and healing to the bones.

Were you surprised or disappointed when Julia's initial gift from David turned out to be a bracelet instead of an engagement ring? How would *you* have responded?

_____

_____

_____

_____

When Julia and David pulled up to the Stantons' home, were you as surprise as Julia that David's parents were so wealthy? Why do you think David never mentioned it before to Julia?

_____

_____

> **Proverbs 23:12 (NLT)**
> Commit yourself to instruction; listen carefully to words of knowledge.

> Her first day at the Stantons' house, Julia wasn't the only one treated rudely by David's mother. She was unkind to her husband and son as well. Their practice of ignoring Gloria's bad behavior was actually reinforcing it—making everyone miserable in the process. Julia was the one who opened David's eyes to their error. Instead of rejecting what she said, he received it as insightful and truly appreciated her honesty.

Are you open to receiving instruction from others? When your parents/guardians try to talk things through with you, do you listen and consider what they are saying? Explain your answers.

_____
_____
_____
_____
_____
_____
_____
_____
_____

At one point Julia says, *Clearly, the Stantons celebrated a different Christmas from the Duncans.* What did she mean?

_____
_____
_____
_____

GRAB YOUR JOURNAL and write what you thought of David's proposal.

Chapter 17

The Unexpected

✦ **JULIA NOTICED** that Gloria's mood was better at breakfast. Why do you think that was?

_____

_____

_____

David's mother had planned the luncheon at the country club to communicate to Julia that she was not a good fit for David and inferior to Cynthia in every way. Even so, Julia tried her best to remain gracious throughout the meal.

Proverbs 15:28 (NLT)
The heart of the godly thinks carefully before speaking; the mouth of the wicked overflows with evil words.

1 Peter 3:9 (NLT)
Don't repay evil for evil. Don't retaliate with insults when people insult you. Instead, pay them back with a blessing. That is what God has called you to do, and he will bless you for it.

Regardless of what Gloria said or did during their outing, Julia did everything she could to respond in a Christ-like way. It wasn't easy because the spiteful things that were said about her and David hurt deeply. Even when she confronted Gloria in the car after lunch, Julia tried to speak respectfully to David's mother. She managed to do so until the very end of their conversation, where she found herself saying a little too much.

It's hard to speak kindly to someone who had just insulted you! The verse above gives you a very good reason to do it anyway. What is it?

_____

_____

Have you ever returned an insult with a kind word? What did you say? What happened after you said it?

David was trying to process Julia's hurt feelings and the seriousness of the situation with his mother. To smooth things over with Julia, he tried to downplay what had happened, making excuses for his mom and questioning whether Julia might be overreacting. Were you disappointed with David for doing this or relieved to see he wasn't perfect after all? Explain.

When Julia went to her room, she released the tears she had been holding back. She realized her dad's concerns about Gloria had been valid, that a postponement of her marriage to David was inevitable. Did you agree with her or think she was overreacting? Would you have felt the same way in similar circumstances?

GRAB YOUR JOURNAL and write out your answers to the two questions in the above paragraph.

Chapter 18

Difficult Assignment

❖ **This chapter** is an emotional roller coaster for everyone concerned. Write down what you were feeling for each character while reading it.

___

> Heartbroken, David and Julia were anxious to get her parents' input on their situation. The wisdom of godly parents is invaluable to children of every age.

Proverbs 6:20-22 (CEV)
Obey the teaching of your parents-- ²¹always keep it in mind and never forget it. ²²Their teaching will guide you when you walk, protect you when you sleep, and talk to you when you are awake.

David and Julia were looking for a solution to their problem from an emotional perspective. Her parents helped them to consider a plan from a spiritual perspective.

After hearing what happened, Julia's parents shared some important things to consider. Write down a few of their points below.

___

Humanly speaking, there seemed to be no way for Julia and David to be happily married. However, David believed that God had promised him a life with Julia. Their decision to break their engagement rested entirely on their faith that God would keep His word to David and somehow change Gloria's heart toward Julia.

> **Numbers 23:19 (CEV)**
> God is no mere human! He doesn't tell lies or change his mind. God always keeps his promises.

When Julia and David agreed to break things off until the problem with his mom was resolved, did you agree or disagree? Explain why.

___

What did Julia's grandmother say about their situation that changed Julia's way of thinking and praying?

___

GRAB YOUR JOURNAL and write what you think it means to put a dream "on the altar of sacrifice."

Chapter 19

Tea Party

❖ **WHAT WAS** the real reason behind Julia's tears as she watched Melody and Flip take their vows?

_____
_____
_____

Julia had to constantly manage her feelings, reminding herself that God was at work and, in His timing, she and David would be together again.

> **Hebrews 10:35-36 (CEV)**
> [35]Keep on being brave! It will bring you great rewards. [36]Learn to be patient, so that you will please God and be given what he has promised.

Did you know?
Staying in faith for something God has promised is a continual fight. Our mind and emotions naturally respond to present circumstances and feelings. This is when we must *will* to believe what God's Word says, even though it hasn't happened yet.

Have you ever been in a situation where believing was sometimes hard, but you stayed in faith and eventually received what God promised you? Explain what happened.

_____
_____
_____
_____
_____

Another man was attracted to Julia in this chapter. Who was he, and what was Julia's response?

___

As Gloria told her story, things were said that could have stirred up past hurts and anger in Julia. However, Julia didn't want to dwell on the past. All she wanted was to quietly listen to what David's mother had come to say.

> **James 1:19 (NLT)**
> Understand this, my dear brothers and sisters: You must all be quick to listen, slow to speak, and slow to get angry.

What did you think of David's conversation with his mother in the treatment center? Did anything he said jump out to you?

___

In her talk with Julia, Gloria said, "I'd accepted Jesus as my Savior, but I'd never made Him the Lord of my life. Truthfully, I had never felt the need."

GRAB YOUR JOURNAL and write what you think Gloria meant by the statement above.

Chapter 20

Gloria's Secret

✦ **How did** Gloria describe her fairy-tale life? What happened to shatter it?

_____
_____
_____

*When Gloria got information regarding an alternative treatment for her daughter's cancer, she dismissed it without **praying or discussing it with her husband**. She eventually regretted it.*

Psalm 86:7 (AMP)
In the day of my trouble I will call on You, for You will answer me.

Proverbs 11:14 (NKJV)
Where there is no counsel, the people fall; but in the multitude of counselors there is safety.

Warning: PRIDE IS DANGEROUS AND COSTLY.
Pride relies on self. Humility relies on God and scriptural advice from godly people.

Thinking we can handle everything on our own sets us up for failure.

Proverbs 16:18 (AMP)
Pride goes before destruction, and a haughty spirit before a fall.

Think honestly for a moment. Is there any area in your life right now that you are stubbornly insisting on handling alone? Can you see how reaching out to God and others is really the better plan? Explain.

_____
_____
_____

James 5:16 (AMP)
Confess to one another therefore your faults (your slips, your false steps, your offenses, your sins) and pray [also] for one another, that you may be healed and restored [to a spiritual tone of mind and heart]. The earnest (heartfelt, continued) prayer of a righteous man makes tremendous power available [dynamic in its working].

It was only when Gloria humbled herself and confessed what she had done that she was set free from her guilt.

Guilt is a heavy load to carry. *How wonderful it feels to admit mistakes and lay down that load!* As we've said before, never feel embarrassed to admit your life is not perfect. *No one's is!* Freedom comes from the truth, and that means *being honest about how things really are*—the good, the bad, and the ugly. By sharing your struggles, weaknesses, and even mistakes with someone else, you can get the prayer, guidance, help, and support you need to continue in God's plan for your life. That plan is too important to miss by hiding mistakes or holding on to guilt.

Were you surprised by Gloria's secret? Did her story give you more compassion for her? Does it help you to see that there's always a reason why people act the way they do? Will that help you when dealing with difficult people? Explain.

_____
_____
_____

What finally ended Gloria's obsession to see David marry Cynthia? How did Gloria end up feeling about Julia?

_____
_____
_____

GRAB YOUR JOURNAL and finish answering the questions above if you ran out of space. Also write about any guilt you may be battling (and then show what you wrote to a trusted adult so he or she can pray with you).

Chapter 21
Heart-to-Heart Talk

✧ **AT LAST** David and Julia were back together again! As they had their heart-to-heart talk on the swing out back, David admits that he knows why God required them to break up for a while. What did the Lord show him about himself?

_____
_____
_____
_____
_____
_____
_____
_____

Psalm 139:23-24 (NLT)
²³Search me, O God, and know my heart; test me and know my anxious thoughts. ²⁴Point out anything in me that offends you, and lead me along the path of everlasting life.

While David was separated from Julia, he spent more time reading his Bible and praying. God used these months to help David work through his history with his mother and evaluate his own maturity as a man.

*David thanked Julia for not putting her love for him ahead of her love for God. Although our love for others is important to the Lord, our love for Him must always come **first**. When it does, everything else works out better.*

Mark 12:30-31 (NIV)
³⁰ "'Love the Lord your God with all your heart and with all your soul and with all your mind and with all your strength.' ³¹The second is this: 'Love your neighbor as yourself.' There is no commandment greater than these."

David impulsively asked Julia to marry him right away. How did Julia answer him? Do you think that later, David was glad they waited? Why or why not.

_____
_____
_____
_____

Explain what happened one summer night when Julia and David were kissing on her backyard swing. How did they decide to modify things from that point on?

_____
_____
_____
_____
_____
_____
_____

When Gloria gifted Carrie's horse, Majesty, to another young rider, she experienced the joy of giving in a new way. Explain.

_____
_____
_____
_____
_____

Julia ends the chapter with, *"I was glad to know that while my husband would have a great deal of money, money would never have him."*

GRAB YOUR JOURNAL and write what Julia meant by the statement above.

Chapter 22

Reality Check

❖ **IN THIS** chapter, Julia is finally planning her wedding! Was it fun watching Julia finally have her turn being the bride-to-be?

Wanting to be beautifully dressed on her wedding day is most every bride's dream—and in the Bible!

> **Revelation 21:2 (NIV)**
> I saw the Holy City, the new Jerusalem, coming down out of heaven from God, prepared as a bride beautifully dressed for her husband.

True to her word, Gloria did not interfere in Julia and David's wedding plans. For what specific reason did Julia try to include Gloria in lots of special ways?

_____
_____
_____
_____

When Gloria came to help Julia select flowers, she stayed at the Duncan house. Why was Julia secretly nervous about that? What did Julia say about rebuilding trust in a relationship?

_____
_____
_____
_____
_____
_____
_____

After her personal shower, Julia had a talk with her mom about her upcoming wedding night. She also went to lunch with her grandmother and talked with her about becoming a wife. Write what you learned or what stood out to you from those two conversations.

_____
_____
_____
_____
_____
_____
_____
_____
_____
_____

While you were watching Julia prepare for her wedding, were you aware that Julia was actually still trapped in her car? Or had you totally forgotten that?

_____
_____

> Julia was hoping to be rescued much sooner than she was. No doubt this trial she was going through seemed to be taking forever!

When trials linger, if we continually cast our cares on the Lord, He will strengthen us and not allow us to be shaken.

Psalm 55:22 (NIV)
Cast your cares on the LORD and he will sustain you; he will never let the righteous be shaken.

GRAB YOUR JOURNAL and write to the Lord, casting your current cares on Him.

Chapter 23

Blessing in Disguise

❖ **WHEN JULIA** awoke the next morning, she didn't just sit in the car and hope for the best. She was trusting God to rescue her, but she was also using anything at her disposal to draw someone's attention to her—her voice, David's watch, etc. How did *you* think Julia would eventually be found?

_____
_____
_____
_____

*God will often ask us **to use what is in our hand**, just as He did Moses at the burning bush and Red Sea. When we obey and do what we can, God does what we cannot.*

Exodus 14:15-16 (NIV)
[15] Then the LORD said to Moses, "Why are you crying out to me? Tell the Israelites to move on. [16] Raise your staff and stretch out your hand over the sea to divide the water so that the Israelites can go through the sea on dry ground."

When Julia was pinned under her steering wheel, she vowed she would walk away from that accident praising God—and she did!

Psalm 56:13 (NIV)
For you have delivered me from death and my feet from stumbling, that I may walk before God in the light of life.

Driving back to Weston in the motorhome, David explained how he and Julia's family found her. What was your favorite part of Julia's rescue?

_____
_____

_____

_____

_____

_____

_____

_____

_____

> **Psalm 91:14 (CEV)**
> The Lord says, "If you love me and truly know who I am, I will rescue you and keep you safe.

What was the *blessing in disguise* regarding Julia's accident? Does it help you to see that sometimes we have the wrong perspective of things in our lives? Explain your answer.

_____

_____

_____

_____

_____

_____

_____

_____

_____

_____

GRAB YOUR JOURNAL and write what you thought of the words Julia had inscribed on the back of David's watch.

Chapter 24
Saying ... *I do*

❖ AS A freshman at Tyler University, Julia almost lost her virginity *and* her life. That harrowing experience caused her to reevaluate her priorities. She realized that her superficial relationship with God needed to change. When she returned home to Weston to continue school, she committed to diligently seek Jesus as her *first* love and top priority. Has Julia's story inspired you to do the same thing? Explain.

_____
_____
_____

> **Hebrews 11:6 (NKJV)**
> But without faith it is impossible to please Him, for he who comes to God must believe that He is, and that He is a rewarder of those who diligently seek Him.

> Putting God first enabled Julia to overcome years of loneliness as well as many challenges and disappointments. In this chapter, her dedication and hard work paid off. God's reward came—she married Mr. Right, the man she'd prayed for and dreamed about for so long. God will do the same for you if you let Him!

So, what did you think of David, Julia's *Mr. Right?*

_____
_____
_____
_____
_____
_____

> David kept his sexual passions for Julia under control during their courtship and engagement. Although this book is fiction, Scripture records Jacob's ability to control his sexual passions for Rachel during the **seven years** he was required to labor before marrying her. If a Christian man **truly loves both God and you**, he will wait for sex until you are married.

> **Genesis 29:18-20 (CEV)**
> [18]Since Jacob was in love with Rachel, he answered, "If you will let me marry Rachel, I'll work seven years for you." [19]Laban replied, "It's better for me to let you marry Rachel than for someone else to have her. So stay and work for me." [20]Jacob worked seven years for Laban, but the time seemed like only a few days, because he loved Rachel so much.

> **To learn more about Jacob and Rachel's love story, read Genesis 29:1-28.**

Were you glad the Rescue Squad from Tyler was at Julia's wedding? How did Kenny's patience pay off?

_____

_____

_____

What did you think of the novel's ending?

_____

_____

_____

_____

_____

_____

GRAB YOUR JOURNAL and write which of the three **Mr. Right Series** novels was your favorite (and why).

You made it!

We are **so proud of you** for working your way through all the issues presented in the **Mr. Right Series Workbook**. Were there more than you expected?

We pray that as we have shared from our current understanding of the Bible, you have been able to receive instruction, encouragement, hope, healing, and a **bigger vision for what God has for your life** today and in the years to come. He loves you so much! We pray our workbook has helped you understand and feel His love on a deeper, more personal level.

We also hope journaling your thoughts to God has helped you to develop better communication with Him, and that the Bible verses given have shown you **how God can talk to you about life** and the things you face every day.

Now that this experience is completed, **you have a choice to make**: to continue your journey with God through more Bible study, prayer, and even journaling if you want, or to simply let your relationship with Him be pushed to the back burner of your life. The decision is yours. We hope you will **choose to keep Jesus as your first love**, to grow in Him more than ever, leaving the past behind and moving on to all that lies ahead in Christ.

We want you to know that while we may not know you personally, we love you in Christ and are praying for you as you face the challenges to come. Remember that **you are never alone!** God is always with you, and He has people everywhere that love Him and will be there for you if you seek them out.

We would love to further connect with you on our website: **www.MrRightSeries.com**. There you will find videos, series news, and our **blog for teen girls and women**. Please write to us and let us know how Julia's story has impacted your life.

May your Heavenly Father take care of you in every way, and may you find joy in trusting and serving our mighty God.

With much love,

Lisa Raftery & Barbara Precourt

Accepting Christ

Before going through this workbook, was your spiritual life important to you? Did you already know that God loves you and wants to be close to you—or did the relationship that Julia and her friends had with God seem strange or unattainable? Maybe no one has told you before how much you mean to God.

The Bible says in John 3:16-18: "God loved the world so very, very much that He gave His only Son. Because He did that, everyone who believes in Him will not lose his life, but will live forever. God did not send His Son into the world to judge the world. He sent Him to save the world. Everyone who believes in the Son will not be judged. But everyone who does not believe in Him is judged already, because He does not believe in the name of God's only Son." (Worldwide English Version)

These verses tell us that God wants *everyone* to be in His family. Yet not everyone will be. We are all born with a sinful nature that separates us from a Holy God—and a sin debt that is too great for anyone to pay. That's why Jesus paid that debt for us on the cross. He paid what we could not. And now we have access to God the Father once again. All that remains is our choice to accept or reject His offer of salvation.

So, if you have never accepted Jesus as your Savior and Lord, you have a decision to make. Ask yourself: *Do I want to run my own life, miss heaven, and experience less than God's best for me right now? Or do I want to receive what Christ did for me and allow God to direct my life from this day forward, letting Him heal my past hurts and design a better future for me?* This choice is yours to make.

If you've already given your life to Jesus and received Him as *Savior*, you have His promise of eternal life in heaven. But it is important to make Christ the *Lord* of your life as well. When Jesus is your Lord, you seek God's will for your life, taking the time to pray, read the Bible, and then *do* what He tells you (to the best of your ability). As you honor God in this way, you will remain under the protective umbrella of His truth and provision. And you will experience the abundant blessings that come through simple faith, trust, and obedience. If you resist this part, however, you will miss out on much of God's best for your life.

How to Receive Jesus as Savior and Lord

If you have never given your life to the Lord but would like to, He is ready and willing to receive you. If you will pray this prayer from your heart, He will give you a new heart that wants to love and serve Him.

> *Heavenly Father, I come to you in Jesus' name and ask You to forgive me for the things I have done wrong and for wanting to live life my own way. Right now I invite Jesus to come into my heart and take control of my life. I believe that He died on the cross to pay for my sins: past, present and future. I believe that He was raised from the dead and will welcome me in heaven when my earthly life is over. Please help me to live for You and for others. I believe You have heard my prayer and that I have been born of Your Spirit. I confess Jesus as my Lord and Savior, and I am now a Christian, one who follows Christ.*

If you have prayed this prayer for the first time or are rededicating your life to the Lord, you need to find a church that teaches the Bible and will help you grow in your relationship with God. You won't be able to reach your full potential without the help of other Christians.

Learn from Julia. She went to church but didn't make the effort to get to know God for herself. The best way to do that is to set aside time to study your Bible and pray. Journaling is another way to connect with God as you record your thoughts and prayers. Over time you can see how you've grown and how God continues to take care of you.

Ideas for Time Spent with God

Some people don't spend time alone with God because they're unsure of what to do. They don't know where to start reading the Bible or how to keep on task. Here are six simple ideas for your time spent with God:

1) Get a blank journal and **continue to write letters to God**, expressing your thoughts, concerns, and what you're learning as you read the Bible. **Copy down favorite verses.** Then talk to God about them in prayer. **Record your prayer requests** so you can go back and check them off as He answers them. When you eventually use up that journal, flip back through the pages. As you review your entries, you'll see how faithful God has been to keep His promises to you. You'll also realize how much more you've grown to love and trust Him.

2) Take time to **pray each day**. It's hard to be close to someone that you never communicate with, so make this a priority. Prayer doesn't mean giving a perfect, elaborate, or lengthy speech. Praying is simply talking to God from your heart.

3) There are 31 chapters in the book of **Proverbs**. You can read **one chapter a day**, according to whatever the date is. If it's June 5, then read Proverbs 5 that day.

4) You can **read through the Gospels** of the New Testament (Matthew, Mark, Luke, & John), **paying special attention to Jesus' words**. Take the thoughts and phrases that mean the most to you and record them in your journal.

5) Find a **one-year Bible** that gives you sections to read daily. You can finish the whole Bible in one year, or if you want to make it simpler, you could read the New Testament sections only, making it two times through the New Testament in one year. This can be done in as little as ten to fifteen minutes a day!

6) Each month you can pick a **book from the New Testament** (like Ephesians, for example) and read **a chapter a day** from it. You may read through the whole book a few times that month, but you'll get a better understanding of what God is saying in those verses.

Whatever you choose to do, have fun with it! Be consistent, and you'll see that time spent with God will literally change your life!

Need more help? Get it!

DON'T TRY TO HANDLE THINGS ON YOUR OWN...

In this workbook, we have worked through some important issues together. If in doing this, you've realized that you need more assistance to deal with the situations in your life—past or present—*please seek professional help.*

Maybe someone in your life is hurting you. Maybe you are hurting yourself. Perhaps you just need to talk to someone about the things you wrote in this workbook. If so, it is important that you *get help now.* There are people all around you that want to see you have the best life possible. You can talk to a *parent, teacher, neighbor, leader at church, or another trusted adult in your life.* They can help get you to a safe place, emotionally and physically.

Remember what we said in this workbook? If you hide your problems or hurts from others, that secrecy will give them cover to grow. If you tell someone about them, however, the light of the truth will expose what's happening, and you can get the help you need to be healed and free. Never feel embarrassed to admit that your life isn't perfect. *No one's life is.* We all need help from others sometimes. *The sooner you seek out help, the sooner you can begin to experience the life God wants you to live!*

> **Jeremiah 29:11 (NLT)**
> "For I know the plans I have for you," says the Lord. "They are plans for good and not for disaster, to give you a future and a hope."

God loves you and wants you to be safe and healthy *in every way.* **Don't wait to get help if you need it.** God wants things to start changing for you *today!*

> **Always call 911 for immediate and real danger.**

www.ingramcontent.com/pod-product-compliance
Lightning Source LLC
LaVergne TN
LVHW051551070426
835507LV00021B/2515